WAVES OF WISDOM

Flow with Life, Grow with Grace

Compiled, Crafted and Curated By

DR. HARI CHINTHAKUNTA

INDIA · SINGAPORE · MALAYSIA

ISBN
Paperback 979-8-89777-938-3
Hardcase 979-8-89906-978-9

WAVES OF WISDOM"

(Flow with Life, Grow with Grace)

Interpretation of PEARLS OF WISDOM
of **His Holiness Sri Vidya Narayana Theertha**
Sri Jagadguru Shankaracharya Samsthanam,
Dwaraka Badarikashram, and Sri Vidya Narayana Foundation,
Bangalore

Compiled, Crafted, and Curated by
Dr. Hari Chinthakunta

**With Divine Grace and Blessings from His Holiness Sri
Vidyanarayana Thirtha**

A HUMBLE DEDICATION

**At the Lotus Feet of the Eternal Guide:
A Humble Dedication to the Mystic Circle of Divinity**

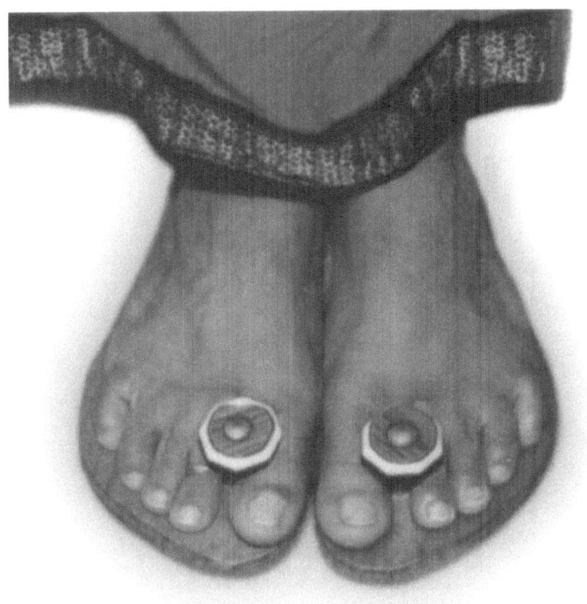

His Holiness Sri Vidya Narayana Theertha
Sri Jagadguru Shankaracharya Samsthanam,
Dwaraka Badarikashram, and Sri Vidya Narayana Foundation,
Bangalore

CONTENTS

HARMONY IN LIFE — 101

Integrating Spiritual Values into Daily Existence to Cultivate Peace and Fulfilment

THE PATH OF DEVOTION   195

(Exploring Faith, Surrender, and the Transformative Power of Devotion)

KARMA AND DHARMA   243

(A Deep Dive into Righteous Action and Onne's Duty in the Grand Cosmic Order)

Contents

ACKNOWLEDGEMENTS

With deep reverence and gratitude, I bow before **Lord Vinayaka**, the remover of obstacles, seeking His divine grace to clear my path of all hindrances and bless

me with wisdom and clarity. To **Lord Subramanyeswara**, I offer my prayers for strength, courage, and discernment, trusting in His divine protection as I embark on this journey of wisdom and growth.

With profound devotion, I surrender to **Goddess Bala Tripura Sundari**, the embodiment of divine grace, whose love nurtures the soul and guides it toward higher consciousness. May Her sacred light illuminate the hearts of all who

seek wisdom. I also invoke the blessings of **Lord Venkateshwara**, the Lord of Seven Hills, praying for His divine presence to instil unwavering faith and devotion in my heart.

I extend my deepest gratitude to the **Saints, Sages, and Seers** of the sacred spiritual lineage, whose wisdom has been a guiding force throughout history. Their eternal presence continues to inspire and uplift all who walk the path of spiritual realization.

My heartfelt appreciation is dedicated to my **divine parents, Avadootha Nanna and Karunamayi Amma**, whose unconditional love and guidance have shaped my journey. I am also deeply grateful to my **divine sister, Sai Niveditha, and my brothers, Naga Yogi Raj and Balayogi Ganesh**, for their unwavering support and encouragement.

Above all, my eternal gratitude is dedicated to my revered Gurudev, His Holiness Sri Vidyanarayana Theertha Swamy. Swamiji's life is truly extraordinary—an embodiment of wisdom, resilience, and unwavering dedication to the path of sanyasa. With

five decades of ascetic life, he has navigated diverse experiences, adapting to various people, situations, and hardships, yet never compromising the fundamental principles and dharma of a renunciate. His impartial love and kindness have embraced all devotees alike, transcending barriers of caste, creed, and background.

Swamiji's compassionate heart radiates warmth, his blessings uplift all who seek his guidance, and his independence is reflected in the simplicity with which he leads his life. His journey is a testament to the profound beauty of living with contentment, detachment, and unwavering faith. His experiences serve as a guiding light, showing us how to cultivate inner peace and embrace life with grace.

His divine presence is the unseen force behind every thought and word in this book. It is through his boundless inspiration that Waves of Wisdom has taken shape, offering seekers a way to flow with life's currents and grow in wisdom. His teachings have illuminated my understanding that life, like the ocean, moves in waves—some gentle, some fierce—but always guiding the soul toward deeper wisdom, resilience, and spiritual fulfilment.

This book is a humble offering, a tribute to the sacred wisdom that allows us to surrender to the rhythm of life and evolve with grace. May it serve as a guiding light for those seeking clarity, peace, and a deeper connection with their own inner truth.

A special acknowledgement is due to Bhagwan Sri Ram SIR, who is everything to me—an unseen yet ever-present guide, a beacon of wisdom, and a force that silently shapes my path. His divine presence transcends words, instilling a sense of purpose and clarity in my journey. To me, 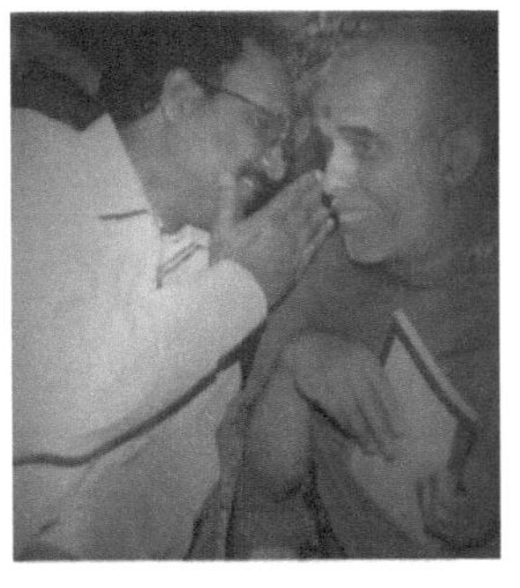 he is not just a mentor but a god incarnate, whose boundless grace and wisdom flow effortlessly, like the eternal waves of life, guiding me toward realization and truth.

A moment of profound revelation struck when someone shared a photograph of Swamy with SIR before I even began compiling the book. It was a shock—an enigma beyond my comprehension— for I had no knowledge of when or how they had met.

Yet, the image spoke volumes, unveiling a deeper reality: the unseen threads that weave together great souls across time and space. The traditional lineage, the silent confluence of their spirits, and the mystic interconnectivity of their journeys reaffirmed the truth that destiny moves in ways beyond human understanding. Some connections are not forged in this lifetime alone—they are eternal, bound by the will of the divine.

With immense gratitude, I extend my heartfelt thanks to **Sree Lekha and Sai Leela**, whose unwavering support has been a pillar of strength in this endeavour. I am also deeply grateful to **Mrs. Konanki Lakshmi Kala**, whose meticulous attention to detail in proofreading has ensured the purity and clarity of this work.

With boundless love and gratitude,

– Dr. Hari Chinthakunta

A SACRED DIALOGUE WITH SWAMY'S SPIRIT

THE SILENT ECHO OF WISDOM

In the stillness of contemplation—where the restless mind surrenders and the soul aligns with the eternal—His Holiness Sri Vidyanarayana Theertha's wisdom flows like a sacred river. His words are not just philosophical musings but living currents of truth, simple in form yet infinite in depth. They echo the wisdom of our ancient scriptures, guiding the seeker beyond intellectual understanding into direct realization.

When Swamy handed me the booklet *Pearls of Wisdom* during my visit to Bangalore in December 2024, it was not a mere exchange of a book. He held it with the reverence of one holding something sacred. "This," he said, "is *Vidya Narayana Geetha*—not just words, but a scripture of wisdom." His instruction was clear: "Do not merely read. Contemplate. Absorb. Let it dissolve the illusions within you."

At first, the teachings seemed deceptively simple. But as I reflected, I encountered the paradox all seekers face—what appears accessible often remains elusive, and what seems profound resists immediate understanding. True wisdom does not yield to mere intellect; it unveils itself only to those willing to surrender.

WISDOM BEYOND WORDS

This struggle reminded me of the sacred discourses in our epics—the *Bhagavad Gita*, where Krishna imparts divine truth amidst the battlefield of duty and doubt; the *Shanti Parva*, where Bhishma reveals dharma as both law and liberation; and the *Yoga Vasistha*, where Rama receives the vast revelations of consciousness. These were not passive conversations; they were transformative encounters meant to dissolve ignorance and ignite realization.

Swamy's words carried the same potency. They were not meant to be analyzed but experienced, not just understood but lived. And just as Arjuna, Yudhishthira, and Rama were guided beyond their limitations, so too was I drawn into an inner dialogue that transcended thought and led into silence, where wisdom is truly absorbed.

THE LIVING PRESENCE OF A MASTER

Almost every day, Swamy calls to check on the progress of this work. To my astonishment, he had already foreseen whatever I intended to write. His words often pre-empt my thoughts as if he were dictating from a realm beyond time. It was not mere intuition—it was the expression of a ripened *siddhi*, a mastery beyond the limits of the mind. His wisdom was not just exceptional; it was boundless.

Realizing this, I arranged the teachings thematically—each section beginning with a reflection, followed by Swamy's words, and finally, my silent dialogue with his spirit. This was my humble attempt to bridge the finite with the infinite, the seen with the unseen, the spoken with the unspoken.

A MASTER'S CALL TO AWAKENING

This book is not a commentary—it is a transmission. Just as the *Ramayana* was not confined to history but flowed as divine revelation through Valmiki's realization, so too does Swamy's wisdom continue beyond the written word. His presence does not fade; it lingers in the stillness of our hearts, in the sacred whispers of intuition, in the moments where truth reveals itself without speech.

A true Master does not merely teach—he ignites. His words are not to be admired but lived. Swamy's wisdom is not a philosophy to be debated; it is a fire that burns ignorance, a light that dissolves illusion. Whether in physical form or beyond, his presence is a call to awakening.

This is not just a dialogue between a disciple and a Master; it is an eternal conversation between the seeker and the Supreme. It belongs to all who thirst for truth, to those searching for clarity amidst the illusions of the world. Every question posed is one that has troubled seekers across time; every answer received is a pearl of wisdom waiting to illuminate the path of the sincere.

May these words inspire you—not just to read but to listen. Not just to know but to realize. For wisdom is not something we acquire; it is something we remember. The seeker does not truly 'learn'—they awaken to a truth that has always been present, waiting to be unveiled.

Let this dialogue serve as a bridge—between the known and the unknown, the seen and the unseen, the transient and the eternal. May it guide you toward the inner light, where the spirit of Swamy eternally dwells, offering wisdom, grace, and boundless love.

– Dr. Hari, Chinthakunta

PREFACE

"The waves may rise and fall, but the ocean remains the same."

– Adi Shankaracharya.

Life is an ever-moving ocean—vast, mysterious, and unpredictable. **Waves rise and fall, tides shift, and the restless surface conceals the depth of profound stillness beneath.** We sometimes struggle against the current, trying to control what is beyond our grasp. But those who truly understand life **do not fight the waves—they learn to flow with them.**

The journey of wisdom is much like the ocean's rhythm. Every wave represents **an experience, a realization, or a lesson** that deepens our understanding. Some waves are gentle, bringing peace; others are fierce, testing our endurance. Yet, **all waves serve a purpose**—shaping, refining, and elevating us.

In moments of struggle, **do we resist and exhaust ourselves, or do we surrender and rise gracefully?** This book invites you to embrace life's waves, navigate its depths, and discover **the unshakable truth within.**

Waves of Wisdom: Flow with Life, Grow with Grace

This title encapsulates the essence of wisdom—**fluid, adaptive, and deeply transformative.** Wisdom is not stagnant knowledge but **a living force that flows through every experience, revealing the deeper truths of existence.** The key lies in understanding two vital principles:

1. **Flow with Life – The Art of Adaptability**

   - **Life is movement**—to resist it is to suffer; to flow with it is to find peace.

   - Like water shaping itself into any vessel, **a wise soul embraces change humbly.**

   - Just as rivers carve new paths when faced with obstacles, **we, too, must find our way through difficulties instead of stopping.**

2. **Grow with Grace – Evolving Through Understanding**

   - Growth is not forced—it is **a natural unfolding, like a flower blossoming in its own time.**

   - Grace is **the wisdom to accept life's lessons with patience, gratitude, and balance.**

   - True evolution occurs when we integrate knowledge with **compassion, humility, and inner strength.**

An Index for Confused Minds: A Roadmap to Clarity

Many of us find ourselves **overwhelmed by information yet starved for true wisdom.** In an age of distractions, spiritual truths serve as **a guiding light, helping us navigate confusion and rediscover purpose.** This book is structured as **a journey through key themes,** each offering a different facet of wisdom:

1. **The Ocean of Wisdom – Realizing Knowledge as a Divine Flow**

   ⊲ Wisdom is not **accumulation** but **awakening**—it is already within you, waiting to be realized.

   ⊲ Like the ocean, **true wisdom remains undisturbed by the surface-level turbulence of life.**

2. **Harmony in Life – Finding Peace Amidst Chaos**

   ⊲ The world moves fast, but **peace is found in stillness, not speed.**

   ⊲ A wise life is one that **balances action with inner silence, duty with devotion.**

3. **The Path of Devotion – Transforming Life Through Surrender**

   ⊲ Faith is **not blindness but inner vision.**

   ⊲ Surrender does not mean weakness—it means **trusting the Divine current to carry us where we are meant to be.**

4. **Karma and Dharma – The Cosmic Balance of Action and Duty**

   ⊲ Every action has a ripple effect—**are your choices aligned with higher truth?**

   ⊲ Dharma is **not a burden—it is a compass guiding us toward our highest purpose.**

A Simple Analogy to Carry With You

Imagine yourself standing at the shore:

   🌊 **If you resist the waves, they knock you down.**

   🌊 **If you flow with them, you learn to surf.**

   🌊 **Over time, these waves shape you, making you stronger, wiser, and more resilient.**

This book is **not just words on a page—it is an invitation** to step into the ocean of wisdom, to move with its rhythm, and to find **the eternal truth that lies beyond fleeting experiences.**

His Holiness Sri Vidyanarayana Theertha, whose guidance illuminates this work, does not offer mere intellectual philosophy—**he embodies wisdom as a lived experience.** Rooted in the unbroken lineage of the Rishis, his words hold the power to dissolve confusion, uplift seekers, and **lead them toward self-realization.** My role in this endeavour is but a humble one—to gather the sacred wisdom he so generously imparts and present it in a way that resonates with modern readers.

As Saint Thiruvalluvar wisely said:

"A wise man, though he reads no books, will find the true path; a fool, though he reads many, will remain ignorant."

May this book not merely be read but **experienced**. May its reflections **stir something deep within you—**a longing to know, to seek, and ultimately, to realize **the boundless ocean of wisdom that has always been within you.**

– **Dr. Hari, Chinthakunta**

DIVINE PRELUDE

WAVES OF WISDOM: FLOW WITH LIFE, GROW WITH GRACE

Life moves like the vast ocean—sometimes calm, sometimes turbulent—but always flowing. Wisdom, too, is not something to be hoarded; it is an ever-moving current, shaping the seeker who surrenders to its depth. True wisdom is not in words alone but in the silent transformation it brings. **"Waves of Wisdom"** is not merely a book—it is a **sacred tide of insight**, meant to carry the sincere seeker beyond the shores of intellectual knowledge into the ocean of direct realization.

For over three decades, **Dr. Hari**, a devoted disciple of **His Holiness Sri Vidyanarayana Theertha**, has been collecting and safeguarding the timeless teachings of Swamy—wisdom that flows effortlessly from a realm beyond the seen and the spoken. Swamy, a mystic saint whose presence defies definition, is not merely a teacher but a **living embodiment of boundless grace**, accessible to both the scholar and the commoner alike. His words are not bound by time; they resonate across generations, awakening those who are ready.

Swamy's guidance is never a mere exchange of knowledge—it is a transmission of truth. Long before this book took form, he had entrusted **Dr. Hari** with the responsibility of preserving these pearls of wisdom. When he first shared his teachings, it was not just an act of sharing but an invitation into deeper knowing. **Holding the scriptures with reverence, he said, "This is not ink on paper; it is Vidya Narayana Geetha—a call to realization."** His words were never meant to be passively read but to be **contemplated, absorbed, and lived**.

"Waves of Wisdom" captures this essence—not as a collection of teachings but as a **living presence, a gentle yet powerful current urging the seeker forward.** It is a work of devotion, shaped by **Dr. Hari's unwavering commitment and selfless service as a Karma Yogi.** His dedication is not merely an initiative—it is a divine invocation, undertaken with humility and complete surrender. **My heartfelt regards to His Holiness Sri Vidyanarayana Theertha for entrusting him with this sacred task.**

A true Master's wisdom does not fade with time—it lingers in the stillness, in the sacred whispers of intuition, in the spaces where truth reveals itself without speech. **May these "Waves of Wisdom" touch every reader, not just as words, but as an experience—guiding each soul to flow with life, grow with grace, and awaken to the eternal truth that has always been within.**

– **Naga Yogi Raj, Monk, Himalayas**

MYSTIC DAWN

SACRED CURRENTS: A JOURNEY INTO LIVING WISDOM

"The wise see knowledge and action as one; they see truly."

— Bhagavad Gita (5:4)

Life, like an eternal river, carves its path through valleys of joy and turbulence, never stagnant, always moving forward. True wisdom mirrors this flow—it is not a possession to be hoarded but an essence to surrender to. It does not reside in mere words but in the silent transformation it ignites. This work is not just a book; it is a  confluence of timeless insights, inviting the seeker beyond the realm of intellect into the vastness of direct realization.

For decades, Dr. Hari has walked the path of unwavering devotion, preserving the luminous teachings of His Holiness Sri Vidyanarayana Theertha. His Holiness is not confined to definitions—he is neither merely a teacher nor a philosopher, but a boundless presence, a bridge between the known and the ineffable.

His wisdom, unshackled by time, does not instruct—it awakens. It does not inform—it transforms.

A mystic saint for over 35 years, **Sri Vidyanarayana Theertha embodies simplicity while carrying the depth of the eternal**. His teachings are unadorned yet profound, his words few but his communication vast. He moves through life with a natural ease—**jovial in demeanor, yet delivering messages that stir deep contemplation**. Rooted in an inner journey that knows no pause, he remains ever accessible to those who seek him, inspiring them not with grand declarations, but with an unshakable presence that speaks beyond words. As the Upanishads declare, *"He who knows the Self transcends all sorrows and delights in the eternal."*

When these teachings were first entrusted to Dr. Hari, it was not merely an offering of knowledge; it was an invitation into deeper seeing. Swamy once said, *"Wisdom is not written; it is realized. It is not spoken; it is absorbed."* Every word in this work carries that intent—not to be read passively, but to be imbibed, to become a lived experience.

> *"The purpose of wisdom is to guide, not to impose;*
> *to illuminate, not to overshadow."*
>
> — *Mahabharata*

This book is not a static compilation but a **dynamic force—a river of insight that continues to flow, carrying seekers toward their own awakening**. Dr. Hari's dedication to this sacred task is not an act of preservation; it is an act of surrender. My deepest reverence to His Holiness for placing this responsibility in his hands, and my heartfelt appreciation for his steadfast service as a Karma Yogi.

May this sacred current reach every soul, dissolving boundaries, deepening awareness, and guiding each reader to **not just witness wisdom—but to live it.**

— Yogini Sai Niveditha

RIPPLES OF INSIGHT: A JOURNEY THROUGH TIMELESS WISDOM

Life, like a flowing river, is ever-changing—sometimes gentle, sometimes fierce, yet always moving toward a greater expanse. True wisdom does not remain stagnant; it moves, deepens, and transforms those who embrace it. Knowledge may fill the mind, but wisdom shapes the soul. *Ripples of Insight* is not just a book—it is an invitation to journey beyond the surface of words and experience the depth of inner realization.

For decades, Dr. Hari has been a dedicated disciple of His Holiness Sri Vidyanarayana Theertha, absorbing and preserving the invaluable teachings of a Master whose wisdom knows no boundaries. Swamy is not confined to tradition—his presence speaks to the scholar and the seeker alike, offering guidance that is both profound and practical. His words are not lessons to be memorized but truths to be lived.

This book is the fruit of a sacred trust, a collection of insights meant to awaken clarity and purpose in the reader's life. Swamy once said, *"True learning is not about collecting thoughts; it is about dissolving illusions."* With this spirit, *Ripples of Insight* does not simply convey teachings; it carries the essence of an enlightened presence. Every page invites reflection, every message stirs the heart, and every truth revealed urges the seeker to look within. May these ripples of wisdom reach every soul in search of light, guiding them toward inner harmony and boundless grace.

– Balayogi Gasha

INVOCATION

By His Holiness Sri Vidyanarayana Theertha

"The highest knowledge is not in mere words, but in realization."

— Kanchi Paramacharya

Wisdom is not static—it moves like a wave, flowing through life, dissolving ignorance, and lifting the soul toward higher realization. It is not a treasure to be hoarded but an energy that must be lived, expressed, and shared. Just as the mighty ocean shapes the shore with each rising tide, so too does wisdom refine our understanding, guiding us to flow with life and grow with grace.

The great Rishis and enlightened Masters have always reminded us that true wisdom is not found in mere words or intellect—it is an awakening, a lived experience. The purpose of knowledge is not to burden the mind but to liberate the soul from its limitations. Yet, in today's world, we find ourselves drowning in information but gasping for true understanding. We advance in science and technology, yet remain restless, disconnected, and unfulfilled. If knowledge does not bring clarity, harmony, and inner peace, what is its true worth? Spiritual wisdom is not an option; it is the very foundation of a meaningful life.

Like waves upon the vast ocean, wisdom is ever-moving—reshaping our consciousness, dissolving false identities, and opening the path to higher truth. However, knowledge without purity of heart and sincerity of purpose remains incomplete. The Bhagavad Gita declares: "Shraddhavan labhate jnanam"—only those who seek with faith, patience, and humility are granted the nectar of divine wisdom. It is not confined to a privileged few but is the birthright of every sincere seeker who yearns to rise beyond the transient and embrace the eternal.

Dr. Hari, through his previous works—Beyond Boundaries, Cosmic Mirror, Hidden Radiance, Whispers of Divine Light, and Zero to Zero: The Mystic Circle—has beautifully distilled the essence of deep spiritual truths into words that awaken, elevate, and transform. In Waves of Wisdom: Flow with Life, Grow with Grace, he carries forth this sacred endeavour, not just offering reflections but urging seekers toward self-inquiry, inner refinement, and conscious evolution. His words do not merely inform—they ignite a spark. They do not stop at philosophy—they lead to experience. This book is not just a collection of thoughts—it is a living force, an invitation to surrender to the flow of life, embrace growth with grace, and realize the divine current within.

To the young, the restless, and the searching souls—this book is your guiding light, your steady hand, your whisper of the Divine. The wisdom of our Rishis and Peetadhipathis is not history—it is a living reality awaiting your embrace. May these pages draw seekers with an open heart, an awakened soul, and the readiness to embark on the most sacred journey—the journey inward.

May Waves of Wisdom: Flow with Life, Grow with Grace awaken the dormant divinity within its readers, filling their lives with wisdom, grace, and the radiant light of divine realization.

— His Holiness Sri Sri Sri Vidyanarayana Theertha

THE OCEAN OF WISDOM

(Understanding Wisdom as an
ever-flowing stream of Divine Realization)

Chapter 1

COSMIC PLAY

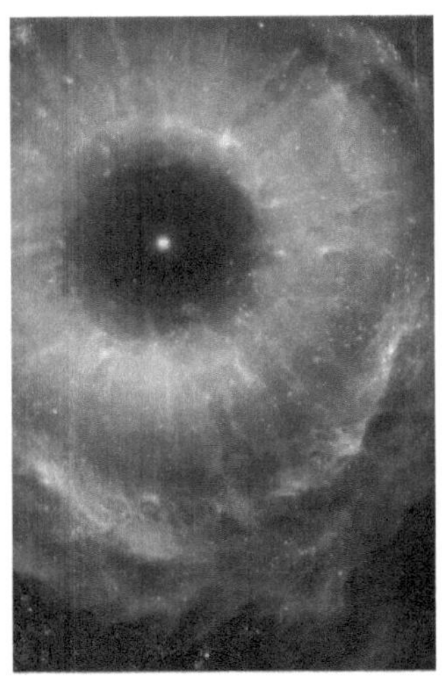

Life is like a grand cosmic play directed by the Divine Mother. Each of us is given a unique role—not by chance, but by her wisdom. Some lead, some support, some create, and some nurture. No role is greater or lesser; each is essential to the story. The script is beyond our understanding, written in the language of the universe. Like a mother who embraces all her children—whether they are white or black, short or tall, beautiful or not, able or disabled, intelligent or dull—the Divine Mother, too, accepts us as we are. The role we play is not new; it is a continuation of the unfinished game from our past lives. The journey of the soul is mysterious, stretching beyond what the mind can grasp. Instead of questioning why, accept it. Instead of comparing, rejoice in what is given. When we stop resisting and truly embrace our part, we feel her love flowing through us. Play your role with joy, and life itself becomes a divine celebration.

Swamy, you said

"Life is a mystery—an unfolding history of joys and sorrows, tragedies and triumphs, complexities and haunting memories, both sweet and bitter. Yet, each moment is a step on the path to the Divine. It is the grand play of the Cosmic Mother, who revels in its unfolding. She instructs me to act with detachment—outwardly engaged, yet inwardly surrendered. She acts through me, making me act. Then who is the owner? Who is the doer? It is all Her."

Swamy, your words are profound, yet they seem to dissolve the very idea of individuality. How does one truly internalize this? How do we act with detachment yet with responsibility? Please guide me to comprehend and live this truth.

Swamy's Spirit Speaks

Child, the moment you **claim ownership, suffering begins**. The moment you **surrender, peace unfolds**. You are neither the doer nor the enjoyer; you are merely an instrument. The river flows not by its will but by the unseen force that guides it.

Let life flow. Let it unfold—without resistance, without attachment.

1. The Cosmic Play—The Dance of the Divine

◁ The **Mother plays, and we are the instruments.**

◁ **Joys and sorrows** are merely chapters in Her grand story.

◁ **Triumphs and tragedies** are Her lessons, shaping the soul. **Complexities and memories** test our wisdom—should we cling or let go?

Each moment, whether painful or blissful, is Her call towards realization.

< **Realizing this truth dissolves the ego, bringing freedom from suffering.**

2. Detachment vs. Responsibility—Living the Wisdom

☝ **Outwardly engaged, inwardly surrendered** – this is the secret.

< **Detachment does not mean indifference.** It means working with sincerity but without anxiety over results.

< **Responsibility does not mean ownership.** It means performing duties as an offering to the Divine without claiming control.

< **True surrender is not weakness.** It is the highest intelligence—knowing that everything happens by a higher design.

💡 **Detach from the fruits, but never from the action itself.**

3. Who is the Doer? The Illusion of 'I'

✗ **The ego whispers:** *"I achieved, I suffered, I created, I failed."*

☑ **The truth is:** *"I am only an instrument; She alone acts."*

When you let go of the 'I', life unfolds effortlessly.

👊 No burden.

👊 No fear.

👊 No struggle.

🐉 **Like waves in the ocean, rise and fall—but always remain One with the Source.**

4. How to Internalize This Truth?

< **Observe:** Watch life unfold without judgment.

< **Surrender:** Accept joy and pain alike, knowing they are Her gifts.

- **Meditate:** Silence the mind; let Her wisdom emerge.
- **Serve:** Offer every action as a prayer, expecting nothing in return.

💡 **When you realize She alone acts, a deep calmness enters your being.**

5. Swamy's Message—The Ultimate Truth

- **You are not the doer; She alone is.**
- **Life is a grand play—watch it, act in it, but do not claim it.**
- **Detachment is not escape; it is mastery.**
- **Surrender is not helplessness; it is power.**
- **Flow with life, for resistance only creates suffering.**

To know this is wisdom. To live this is liberation.

Chapter 2

UNIVERSAL LOVE

Love is not bound by borders, identities, or conditions—it flows like an eternal river from the Divine Mother, embracing all. Just as the sun shines on everyone without asking who is worthy, her love touches every soul, whether kind or cruel, rich or poor, wise or ignorant. Like a mother who cherishes all her children—regardless of their strengths or flaws—she accepts us as we are. The love we receive today is not new; it is the echo of what we have given and received across lifetimes. The journey of love is mysterious, woven into the soul's endless voyage.

Let us come out of the narrow shell of religion, regions, ideologies, and philosophies that shrink our hearts. Let the human touch within us be broadened, for love knows no boundaries. But let us also remember that lust is not love—both are different. The word 'love' is horrifyingly misused, reduced to mere desire, when, in truth, it is something sacred. Lust arises when the senses are in full swing, restless and demanding. But love is when the senses rest peacefully, like a child cradled in the lap of the Divine Mother. True love calms, nurtures, and elevates—it is the highest expression of the soul.

Swamy, you always say,

"I love you all, I thank you all, and I bless you all."

I understand the importance of universal love, gratitude, and blessings, yet I wish to know how you convey this message. What is the deeper essence behind these words, and how can we internalize and express them in our daily lives?

Swamy's Spirit Speaks

Child, these words are a pure expression of divine grace and a reminder of our interconnectedness with all of creation. Let me share their deeper essence with you:

- **Universal Love**
  - ✓ **"I love you all"** is not merely a greeting; it is an affirmation that every soul is a reflection of the Divine.
  - ✓ By saying this, I invite you to open your heart and see beyond superficial differences—recognizing that love is the fundamental bond that unites all beings.
  - ✓ This love is unconditional and all-encompassing; it encourages you to embrace others with warmth and acceptance, nurturing a sense of oneness.
- **Boundless Gratitude**
  - ✓ **"I thank you all"** signifies a deep, heartfelt gratitude for the myriad gifts of life—every joy, every lesson, every encounter.

- ✓ Gratitude is the recognition of the blessings that flow into your life, even through challenges.
- ✓ When you practice gratitude, you open yourself to further grace and cultivate an inner environment where peace and happiness can flourish.

◄ Divine Blessings

- ✓ **"I bless you all"** expresses the conviction that the Divine's grace is available to every soul.
- ✓ Blessings here are not limited to material gain; they encompass the light of wisdom, the comfort of peace, and the strength to overcome adversity.
- ✓ To bless is to send out an energy that heals and uplifts, ensuring that every individual is supported on their journey toward truth.

◄ The Cycle of Grace

- ✓ These words form a cycle—a harmonious interplay where love begets gratitude, gratitude begets blessings, and blessings inspire further love.
- ✓ When you embody this cycle in your life, you become a channel for the Divine, radiating positivity and compassion in all your interactions.
- ✓ This cycle is a reminder that the power to transform your life and the world lies within you; by nurturing these qualities, you contribute to a more unified and enlightened society.

Child, the true essence of my message is to live from a place of inner abundance. When you love without conditions, express gratitude with sincerity, and share blessings selflessly, you align yourself with the eternal flow of divine grace. This alignment not only uplifts your own spirit but also inspires and transforms the lives of others.

May you always feel the warmth of universal love, the depth of heartfelt gratitude, and the empowering touch of divine blessings guiding you to everlasting peace and unity.

Chapter 3

DIVINE UNION

Life compels us to unite with the world—to build relationships, fulfil responsibilities, and play our roles. This union is inevitable, yet it is fleeting. Like a lotus that blooms untouched by the murky waters, we must be detachedly attached— present in the world, yet not bound by it. Love, serve, and engage, but do not lose yourself in the ever-changing tides of existence.

But with the Divine, it is not union—it is communion. A silent merging, where no boundaries remain. Here, there is no attachment, for there is no separation. In the world, you give and take, but in Divine communion, you dissolve. You are no longer an individual seeking God—you become one with Him. When the soul surrenders completely, when the mind ceases its restless grasping, only then does true union dawn. In that moment, you do not just find the Divine— you realize you were never apart.

Swamy, you declare,

"I am the Master, Master is in Me, and I am at His Holy Feet."

What does this truly mean, and how do we understand it from a cosmic perspective?

Swamy's Spirit Speaks

Child, these words are a sacred mirror reflecting the profound interplay between the individual and the Divine. Let me explain their essence:

- **"I am the Master"**
  - ✓ This is not a boast of personal power but an awakening to the truth that the highest potential and wisdom reside within you.
  - ✓ To be the Master means to realize that you are not bound by the limitations of the ego; you are capable of directing your inner energies with clarity and purpose.
  - ✓ It is the call to recognize that your inner self, when purified through discipline and self-inquiry, becomes the guiding force in your life.

- **"Master is in Me"**
  - ✓ This phrase tells you that the Divine, the ultimate source of all wisdom and power, is not external or separate from you—it dwells within your very essence.
  - ✓ Every heartbeat, every thought, every breath is infused with that divine presence. When you awaken to this truth, you discover that you are not merely a transient being but an embodiment of the eternal.

- ✓ The realization that the Master is within you transforms your understanding of self—it dissolves the illusion of separation and reveals the unity of all existence.

- ◄ **"I am at His Holy Feet":**
  - ✓ Here, true surrender is celebrated. Despite the divine power residing within you, there is a call for humility.
  - ✓ To be at His holy feet means to remain ever humble, recognizing that while you are an instrument of divine energy, you are not the source of it.
  - ✓ It is an acknowledgement that the path of self-mastery is not about egoistic pride but about serving the higher truth with gratitude and reverence.

Chapter 4

THE PARADOX OF TRUTH

Truth is eternal, yet it appears different to each one who seeks it. Some perceive it through scriptures, others through reason, and a few through silence. It is spoken in a thousand ways, yet it remains unspoken. Those who cling to words argue over it, while those who have seen it smile in stillness. Truth does not belong to any religion, philosophy, or ideology—it simply is.

But here lies the paradox: the more you chase it, the further it seems. It cannot be grasped, only realized. The mind, eager to claim and define, clouds what the soul already knows. Truth is not in accumulation, but in surrender—not in possessing knowledge, but in dissolving the knower. When the seeking ends, when the self is no more, truth reveals itself—not as something found, but as something that was never lost.

Swamy, on some occasions, you say,

"I am this, I am not this, but I am this. God is very kind."

To a common man, these words may seem contradictory. How should one understand their true meaning?

Swamy's Spirit Speaks

Child, these words are a profound reminder of the journey toward self-realization and the gentle nature of the Divine. Though they may appear paradoxical at first, each phrase holds a distinct insight into the nature of the self and the grace of God. Let me explain:

- **"I am this":**
  - This is an affirmation of the part of you that is empowered by divine potential.
  - It signifies the qualities and strengths you possess when you are in tune with your true, eternal self.
  - In this state, you acknowledge your capacity to act, love, and create—recognizing the divinity that flows through you.

- **"I am not this":**
  - This part reminds you that you are not confined to the limited identity shaped by ego, social labels, or fleeting emotions.
  - It is a call to reject the illusions and false identities that often bind you to suffering and limitation.
  - By declaring "I am not this," you free yourself from attachments and the misperceptions of the conditioned mind.

- **"But I am this":**
  - ✓ This reaffirms your true nature—the unchanging, eternal soul that exists beyond the dualities of existence.
  - ✓ It is the realization that, despite the transient forms and thoughts, there is a core of truth within you that remains pure and constant.
  - ✓ This truth is the basis of your inner strength and wisdom, waiting to be recognized and embraced.

- **"God is very kind":**
  - ✓ This is the gentle reassurance that despite the complexities and contradictions of life, the Divine is compassionate and ever-supporting.
  - ✓ God's kindness means that even as you navigate the tension between the false self and the true self, the Divine continuously showers grace and understanding upon you.
  - ✓ It reminds you that the path of self-realization is nurtured by a loving force that forgives, guides, and sustains you through every struggle.

The Deeper Message

Child, the interplay of these statements teaches you that the journey to self-realization involves both the acceptance and rejection of various aspects of your identity.

- **Embrace what empowers you ("I am this"),** but also recognize and let go of what confines you ("I am not this").

- **Ultimately, realize your eternal self ("but I am this")**, and know that the Divine, in its infinite kindness, supports you unconditionally.

- This awareness helps you transcend the limitations of the ego and live a life of clarity, purpose, and compassion.

May you always seek the truth within, understanding that every contradiction is simply a stepping stone toward a deeper realization. Trust in the gentle kindness of the Divine as you navigate your journey, and let that inner light guide you to a life of profound peace and liberation.

Chapter 5

THE ULTIMATE REFUGE

*In the grand design of existence,
nothing truly belongs to us—
neither wealth, knowledge, nor fleeting
achievements. The restless mind seeks
security in accumulation, but true
refuge is not found in possessions or
recognition. It lies in surrender—acting
without attachment, loving without
conditions, and serving without seeking
reward. Nature whispers this wisdom in
its silent giving: trees offer shade, rivers
nourish, and the sun shines, never asking* 
*for gratitude. Like the vast sky, the awakened soul embraces storms
and sunshine, neither resisting nor possessing. When we let go of the
illusion of control and become instruments of the Divine, we discover
the eternal sanctuary—the peace that needs no validation, the joy
that exists beyond gain and loss, the ultimate refuge where we are
not the doers but the flow itself.*

———•———

Swamy, you often say,

"All ends at the feet of God. Anything and everything finds its fulfilment there. Only the foolish fail to realize this. People ignore seeking refuge at His feet, yet they receive everything—health, peace, and prosperity."

What is the true essence behind this statement, and how should we understand it?

Swamy's Spirit Speaks

Child, this teaching is a profound reminder that the ultimate source of all blessings and fulfilment is the Divine. Let me unfold its deeper meaning for you:

- **All Ends at the Feet of God**
  - This phrase signifies that every aspect of existence—every joy, sorrow, challenge, and triumph—culminates in the Divine.
  - The "feet of God" symbolize a state of surrender and complete reliance on the higher power. In humility, when you seek refuge, life's mysteries are resolved, and true strength is found.
  - Think of it like a river that eventually merges with the ocean. No matter how winding its course, every drop ultimately returns to its source. Similarly, all your endeavours and experiences are designed to lead you back to the Divine.

- **Fulfilment in the Divine**
  - When I say, "Anything and everything finds its fulfilment there," I mean that the complete resolution of your

desires, needs, and aspirations lies in connecting with God.

✓ Health, peace, prosperity, and spiritual joy are not accidental; they are the natural fruits of aligning your life with divine principles.

✓ By seeking refuge at His feet, you open yourself to the infinite grace that transforms and uplifts every aspect of your being.

◅ The Folly of Ignorance

✓ "Only the foolish fail to realize this" serves as a gentle caution. When you neglect to seek the refuge of the Divine, you remain entangled in the transient and often tumultuous play of the material world.

✓ Such neglect leads to missed opportunities for growth and the inner fulfilment that comes from spiritual alignment.

◅ Practical Understanding

✓ **Surrender:** Embrace humility. Understand that despite all your efforts, there is a power greater than you, and true strength lies in surrendering to that force.

✓ **Seek Refuge:** Cultivate a daily practice—be it meditation, prayer, or quiet reflection—that brings you closer to that divine centre.

✓ **Trust in the Process:** Recognize that even when you do not consciously seek it, life bestows upon you the gifts of health, peace, and prosperity when your heart is open to divine guidance.

✓ **Live in Alignment:** When your actions, thoughts, and intentions are aligned with higher truth, every moment becomes a stepping stone towards deeper fulfilment.

Child, the essence of my words is simple yet profound: the ultimate fulfilment of your life is found in the Divine. All your experiences are part of a larger tapestry that leads you back to that sacred centre. When you learn to seek refuge at the feet of God—with humility, trust, and surrender—you tap into a boundless source of grace that nourishes every part of your existence.

May you always have the wisdom to seek the divine in every moment, the courage to surrender, and the grace to experience true fulfilment and peace.

Chapter 6

HEAVEN AND HELL WITHIN

Heaven and hell are not distant places—they exist within us, shaped by how we think, feel, and act. When we fill our hearts with love, gratitude, and kindness, life itself becomes heaven—peaceful, joyful, and fulfilling. But when we let anger, jealousy, and greed take over, we  *sink into a living hell, trapped in our own suffering.*

Hell is not about fire, nor is heaven about golden gates—it is the state of our mind. A restless mind, filled with regret and fear, creates endless turmoil, while a heart that forgives and a mind that stays calm and content will always find peace. Every choice we make, every thought we nurture, builds our reality. Will we create a life of harmony, or will we let negativity pull us into misery? The power lies within us—let us stay alert, choose wisely, and build our own heaven, right here, right now.

Yet, we waste precious time debating these ideas, arguing over theories, and following those who preach but do not practice. Many offer not the sweet juice of wisdom but the dry pulp of empty words. Beware of those who talk of virtue but live in contradiction. True wisdom is not in speeches but in action. Instead of debating heaven and hell, let us focus on living rightly, transforming ourselves, and making the world around us better.

Swamy, when people ask you about peace, you often say with a smile, **"A mind in peace is heaven, a mind in pieces is hell. We should watch our thoughts in our mind."** While we grasp a glimpse of this truth, we fail to measure its depth. Can you clarify?

Swamy's Spirit Speaks

Peace is not something found outside; it is the very nature of an undisturbed mind. **When the mind is whole, still, and in harmony, it becomes heaven—a space of clarity, contentment, and divine presence. But when the mind is fragmented, restless, and burdened by conflicting thoughts, it turns into hell—an endless cycle of confusion, suffering, and distress.**

The difference between heaven and hell is not in some distant world; it is in the **state of your mind.** You live in the reality you create within. If your thoughts are scattered, you will experience turmoil no matter where you are. If your thoughts are calm and clear, even chaos around you cannot shake your inner tranquillity.

That is why I say, **"Watch your thoughts."** Your mind is like a flowing river—if left unchecked, it can flood and destroy, but if guided, it nourishes and gives life. Learn to observe your thoughts without getting entangled in them. **Do not become a slave to what arises in your mind—be the master of your inner world.**

To find peace, stop searching for it in the external world. **It is not in possessions, not in achievements, not even in the absence of difficulties. It is in mastering the art of being still amidst everything.** The moment you realize this, you will see—**heaven was never far, and hell was never near. It was all within you.**

Chapter 7

HARMONIZING ENERGY

*L*ife is a precious flow of energy, yet we often waste it without realizing its value. Nature bestows upon us an abundant force meant to be nurtured, yet we dissipate it through restless distractions. In a world driven by machines and digital screens, we have become mechanical—living through devices rather than true experiences. We depend on cell phones but forget the energy within ourselves, draining our vitality without replenishing it. Human touch, real conversations, and moments of stillness are fading, replaced by endless scrolling and artificial engagement.

Just as nature restores itself through cycles of rest and renewal, we, too, must learn to pause, reflect, and realign. Our energy is not infinite—it must be conserved, nourished, and channelled with awareness. True vitality is not about constant motion but about balance—where action meets rest, and external noise gives way to inner clarity. When we respect *and harmonize our energy, life ceases to be a race toward exhaustion and transforms into a journey of depth, connection, and fulfilment.*

Swamy, on one occasion—though I do not recall exactly when—you said, **"Caste is the** concentration of energy, an energy delicate enough to suit humanity and human tendencies, to have heart, to recognize the superfine energy which is called God. Caste is the distribution of energy to suit human mental attitudes." This seems profound yet difficult to grasp. Could you kindly illuminate its deeper meaning?

Swamy's Spirit Speaks

Caste, in its purest sense, is not about division—it is about the flow of energy, the structuring of divine potential within humanity. Just as the body has different organs, each performing its unique function, society too was once structured based on qualities, tendencies, and the ability to refine and channel energy towards the higher purpose of existence.

When I say caste is a concentration of energy, I mean that every individual carries a unique vibrational essence—a potential that, when harnessed correctly, contributes to the harmony of the whole. However, when this understanding is lost, and the flow of energy is blocked by ignorance and attachment to identity, caste becomes a limitation instead of a liberation.

To recognize caste in its divine essence is to see not separation but specialization—not hierarchy, but harmony. The highest purpose of any classification is to recognize the superfine energy within oneself and others, to refine it, to uplift, and ultimately, to dissolve all distinctions in the oneness of God.

Human tendencies fluctuate, and mental attitudes differ, which is why energies were once channelled in different directions. But when the heart awakens, there is no caste—only consciousness. To live in this realization is to move beyond the seen and enter the realm of truth. Do not cling to the outer form, seek the inner essence. That is where all distinctions disappear, and only the divine remains.

Chapter 8

ESSENCE OF BEING

In the rush of life, we often forget what it truly means to be. We define ourselves by roles, expectations, and achievements, yet something always feels incomplete. The essence of being is not in what we do, but in how deeply we  *connect—with ourselves, with others, and with existence itself. When we pause, free from distractions and judgments, we realize that our worth is not measured by external success but by the peace we cultivate within. The mind, when burdened with fears and comparisons, drifts away from its true nature. But when we embrace stillness, we rediscover clarity, purpose, and the quiet joy of simply being. Life is not about racing ahead or looking back—it is about being fully present, aware, and alive in this very moment.*

Swamy, it is difficult to decipher the meaning behind your words: **"I am this, I am not this, but I am this. God is very kind."** How are these statements connected, and why do they seem paradoxical? Could you clarify their deeper essence?

Swamy's Spirit Speaks

This statement is not a puzzle of words, but a **revelation of existence itself.** It reflects the journey of self-realization, the dance between identity and transcendence.

"I am this"—At the surface, it means **I exist, I perceive, I play my role in this world.** This is the level where one identifies with the body, the name, the responsibilities, and the experiences of life. It is the realm of relative truth, where one acknowledges the part they play in the grand design.

"I am not this"—But deeper awareness awakens, and I realize **I am not limited to this body, this mind, this fleeting identity.** The 'I' that suffers, that rejoices, that clings to the material world is not the true 'I.' This realization detaches me from the illusion of separateness.

"But I am this"—Yet, beyond denial, beyond rejection, I come full circle. **I am all that I see and beyond what I perceive.** I am not bound by identity, but I exist within everything. Like the ocean in the drop and the drop in the ocean, the individual soul and the universal spirit are inseparable. This is the wisdom that reconciles all contradictions.

And finally, **"God is very kind."** Because in this realization, there is no struggle, no conflict—only divine grace. The moment I stop trying to define myself in fragments, the whole truth is revealed. **God's kindness is not in giving answers but in opening the eyes that see.**

To understand this is to break free from the chains of false perception. **It is not a contradiction; it is a journey—one that takes you from illusion to truth, from self to the Self, from 'I am' to 'I am That.'**

Chapter 9

DIVINE DUTY

*D*uty *is not just an obligation but a sacred responsibility, a path to fulfilment and purpose. Yet, in today's world, we often fail in our duties—not because we lack ability, but because we lack awareness. We prioritize convenience over commitment, distractions over discipline, and self-interest over service. True duty is not about performing tasks for recognition or reward; it is about*  *embracing our role with sincerity, whether as a parent, a teacher, a leader, or a seeker.*

When duty is performed with devotion, it transforms work into worship, effort into excellence, and struggle into strength. But when neglected, it leads to chaos—within ourselves and in society.

The world suffers not because of a lack of resources but because of a lack of responsibility. To awaken to our divine duty is to rise above excuses, to serve with integrity, and to understand that every action has the power to uplift or destroy. Let us not wait for inspiration to do what is right; let us act, for in fulfilling our duty, we fulfil our higher purpose.

Swamy, one day, you jovially asked the young, **"Are you beautiful or dutiful?"** and then elaborated, **"Everyone is allotted duty. What is duty? Duty is allotted by divinity. Duty is divine. Human beings claim, but God does not claim."** At first, it sounds simple, yet it carries a deeper complexity. Could you please clarify its true essence and ease my understanding?

Swamy's Spirit Speaks

This question is not about **choosing between beauty and duty,** but about recognizing where true beauty lies. The world often admires external beauty—**a fleeting illusion shaped by form, features, and perception.** But what is real beauty? It is not in the skin but in the **spirit, not in appearance but in action.**

"Everyone is allotted duty." You were not born by accident, nor are you moving through life without purpose. Your duty—be it as a parent, student, teacher, or seeker—is **not a burden, but a sacred responsibility.** It is the silent whisper of the divine, guiding you toward righteousness.

"Duty is allotted by divinity." Your very existence carries a purpose woven into the fabric of creation. **Like the sun that shines without seeking reward, like the river that flows without demanding recognition, true duty is beyond selfish desire.** It is the force that sustains life and harmony.

"Duty is divine." When work is done with **love, sincerity, and selflessness,** it ceases to be a mere obligation and transforms into worship. **God does not claim because He gives.** The tree does not claim the fruits it bears, the ocean does not claim the waves it creates—divinity gives without possession.

The essence of this teaching is simple: **Fulfil your duty with devotion, and beauty will naturally radiate from within you. True beauty is not in being admired but in being useful, not in being noticed but in being noble.** Those who understand this will find that duty itself is the highest form of grace, and **to serve is to shine.**

Chapter 10

POWER WITHIN

*P*ower is not about ruling over others—it is about mastering oneself. True power is not measured by dominance or control but by the ability to create, uplift, and transform. It is the silent force that fuels

wisdom, kindness, and resilience. The strongest people are not those who command fear but those who inspire change.

Yet, in today's world, power is often mistaken for authority, and strength is confused with aggression. But real power is not destructive—it is creative. It does not seek to crush but to build. It is not in loud words but in quiet actions that bring light where there is darkness. When power within is directed toward service, it ceases to be selfish and becomes sacred.

Look around—those who misuse power may appear strong, but they crumble under its weight. Those who channel it for good leave an impact that outlives them. The greatest power is not in conquering the world but in conquering oneself. When you awaken this power *within, it does not enslave—it liberates. It does not oppress—it uplifts. And when aligned with a higher purpose, it does not just change a life—it changes the world.*

Swamy, you often say, **"The more you move in, the more power you gain to enjoy peace, health, and prosperity."** Truly speaking, I struggle to grasp its essence, even when I try to find meaning between the lines. Could you illuminate this for me?

Swamy's Spirit Speaks

This is not a statement to merely hear—it is a truth to **experience.** In life, people search for **peace, health, and prosperity** in the outer world, chasing after wealth, recognition, and security. But what they fail to realize is that **all that they seek is already within them.**

"The more you move in" means the deeper you go within yourself, the more you unlock the infinite source of power. Just as a well-digger finds purer water the deeper he digs, you will discover a greater depth of energy, clarity, and strength when you turn inward. **Peace is not given; it is realized. Health is not just physical; it is the harmony of mind, body, and spirit. Prosperity is not just wealth; it is the richness of being.**

When the mind is restless, scattered outward, peace remains distant. But **when you withdraw from distractions and focus within, peace becomes your natural state.** The same applies to health and prosperity—true well-being comes not from external comforts but from inner alignment. **When your thoughts are pure, when your heart is light, and when your awareness is deep, life flows effortlessly.**

The world tells you to move outward—to seek, to strive, to acquire. But I tell you, **move inward, for there lies the real treasure.** The one who **masters himself needs nothing from the world, yet the world bows before him.** This is not philosophy—it is the eternal law. **Know thyself, and everything else will follow.**

Chapter 11

OMNIPRESENCE

*O*mnipresence refers to the ability to be present everywhere at all times, an attribute often attributed to the divine. In spiritual teachings, omnipresence signifies the boundless, infinite nature of the divine consciousness that permeates all of existence. It is not confined by time, space, or form, and can be felt in every corner of the universe, within all beings, and in every experience. This concept helps us understand that the divine is not separate from us but is present in all things, guiding and sustaining life in unseen and mysterious ways. Omnipresence reveals that we are not alone in the journey of life, as the divine is always with us, even when we may not be aware of it.

From a human perspective, omnipresence teaches us to recognize the interconnectedness of all life. It calls us to see beyond our limited perception of the world, reminding us that we are all part of something much greater. The divine presence is in the air we breathe, the earth beneath our feet, and the people we encounter. It encourages *us to be more present in the moment, to connect with others, and to acknowledge the sacredness in everyday life. Omnipresence encourages us to cultivate awareness and mindfulness, realizing that every action, thought, and word reverberates in the fabric of the universe.*

Spiritually, the awareness of omnipresence invites us to surrender to the divine's guiding hand in our lives. By recognizing that the divine is not far away but within us and around us, we are reminded that there is a deep purpose behind everything. In moments of doubt or difficulty, knowing that the divine is omnipresent can bring comfort, peace, and a sense of security. It invites us to deepen our faith, trust in the unseen, and live with the understanding that everything is happening as part of a larger cosmic design. The divine is always with us, supporting us, and leading us towards greater love, wisdom, and enlightenment.

Swamy, you once said,

"Everywhere is, in everything, at all times, at all places, in each item—see Him, seek His grace, surrender to Him."

Although I understand the essence, I believe your perspective always carries a depth beyond normal comprehension. Please explain the deeper meaning of this statement.

Swamy's Spirit Speaks

Child, this statement is not just a set of words—it is the very foundation of spiritual vision, the essence of divine realization. Let me unfold its significance for you.

◁ **"Everywhere is, in everything"**

The Divine is not confined to temples, scriptures, or rituals. He is not separate from existence. If you believe God is only in one place and absent in another, then your vision is limited. Whether it is the vast sky or a grain of sand, a blooming flower or a fading leaf, every atom pulsates with His presence. He is the seen and the unseen, the manifest and the unmanifest.

◁ **"At all times, at all places"**

Time and space do not bind Him. Whether in joy or sorrow, whether in moments of success or failure, He is present. In a palace or a hut, in the marketplace or the meditation hall— there is no moment or place where He is absent. Recognizing this truth means living with constant awareness, knowing that divinity flows through every experience.

◁ **"In each item—see Him"**

When you look at the world, what do you see? Do you see objects, names, and forms, or do you perceive the divine essence within them? Seeing Him in each item means seeing beyond the outer layer. A pot is not just a pot—it is the clay. A wave is not just a wave—it is the ocean. Similarly, everything you see is not separate from Him. To see the Divine in everything is to transcend superficial distinctions and recognize the unity beneath diversity.

◁ **"Seek His grace"**

Awareness alone is not enough—one must seek His grace. Grace is not something given from outside; it is the awakening of the divine spark within. It is the light that clears ignorance, the force that lifts the soul beyond limitations. Seeking grace means surrendering the ego, humbling the mind, and allowing the Divine to guide your path.

⩤ **"Surrender to Him"**

True surrender is not about weakness—it is about trust. A river does not resist its flow toward the ocean; a bird does not resist the wind that carries it. Likewise, surrendering to Him means aligning your will with His, allowing life to unfold without resistance, fear, or doubt. When you surrender, you do not lose yourself—you become infinite.

The Deeper Essence

This statement is a call to dissolve separateness. It reminds you that God is not far, He is not hidden—He is right here, right now, in and around you. To recognize Him is to shift from mere existence to divine living.

When you start seeing Him in everything, life becomes sacred. When you seek His grace, your journey becomes effortless. When you surrender to Him, you become limitless.

May your eyes always see, your heart always seek, and your soul always surrender.

Chapter 12

BLESSED ABUNDANCE

Blessed abundance is a state where we experience the flow of life's gifts—physical, emotional, and spiritual—in their fullest, most divine expression. It is the 

realization that true abundance is not just about material wealth, but the richness of love, peace, health, wisdom, and fulfilment that can manifest in every aspect of our existence. When we live in alignment with our higher purpose, we open ourselves to receive blessings in every form, recognizing that abundance is not something we chase, but something that flows naturally when we live with gratitude, generosity, and openness.

In a world that often defines abundance by material accumulation, spiritual abundance transcends this understanding. It is about cultivating a mindset of gratitude, where we acknowledge the blessings already present in our lives, big and small. True abundance grows when we focus not on what we lack but on what we have—our talents, relationships, health, and the moments of peace that grace our lives. This perspective shifts our attention away from scarcity and into the abundance that already surrounds us. It is through this lens of gratitude and trust that we become open to receiving even more blessings, as the universe responds to the energy we put out.

Spiritually, blessed abundance also represents a deep connection to the divine. When we are aligned with our higher self and live in harmony with the universal flow, we recognize that abundance is a reflection of divine grace. The divine, in its infinite wisdom, bestows upon us everything we need at the right time. It encourages us to trust that we are always provided for, and that the essence of life is a continuous cycle of giving and receiving. By practicing generosity, whether through time, love, or resources, we increase the flow of abundance, both in our own lives and in the lives of others. Blessed abundance is not just about having more, but about being more— more compassionate, more present, more attuned to the divine presence in every moment.

In embracing blessed abundance, we realize that true wealth is found in our capacity to share, to love, and to experience life with a heart full of gratitude. It is the knowledge that we are part of a larger, interconnected whole, and that the abundance we receive is not ours to hoard but to share, to bless, and to lift others. Through this practice, we invite divine abundance into our lives and allow it to transform us into vessels of generosity, kindness, and joy.

——•◆•——

Swamy, what you mentioned is that blessings bring bountiful peace, health and prosperity. It's true, but I need to hear more from you about why you made such a statement.

Swamy's Spirit Speaks

Child, the phrase "blessings bring bountiful peace, health, and prosperity" is a reminder of the abundant grace available to those who align with the Divine. Let me explain the essence of each word:

- **Blessings**
  - ✓ Blessings are the divine graces and positive energies that flow from the Creator.
  - ✓ They are not earned by force or accumulation but are freely given when you live with sincerity, compassion, and humility.
  - ✓ Blessings manifest as moments of insight, acts of kindness, and unexpected gifts that enrich your life.

- **Bountiful Peace**
  - ✓ This peace is not merely the absence of conflict but a deep, inner calm that permeates your being.
  - ✓ It comes when your mind is clear and your heart is open to the Divine, allowing you to navigate life with serenity regardless of external circumstances.

- **Health**
  - ✓ Health here encompasses not only physical well-being but also mental and spiritual balance.
  - ✓ When you receive blessings, they rejuvenate your body, calm your mind, and strengthen your spirit, creating a state of holistic vitality.

- **Prosperity**
  - ✓ Prosperity is the abundant flow of resources and opportunities—material and spiritual—that arise when you live in harmony with divine principles.
  - ✓ It reflects a life that is rich in love, generosity, and growth, where success is measured not solely by wealth but by the fulfilment of your higher purpose.

How Blessings Are Given

- Blessings are imparted through the natural flow of the universe when you align your thoughts, actions, and heart with truth and love.

- They come as the result of your inner transformation—when you practice kindness, service, and self-reflection, you open yourself to receiving the grace of the Divine.

Who Is Eligible to Receive Them

- Every soul is inherently worthy of blessings.

- However, the key is in your readiness:
  - Cultivate humility and sincere devotion, and be open to learning and evolving.
  - When you let go of ego and attachments, you create space for blessings to flow into your life.

Child, the message is simple yet profound: live in alignment with divine principles—be kind, serve selflessly, and remain humble—and you will naturally attract the blessings of peace, health, and prosperity. They are the gifts of the Divine, freely available to those who are open-hearted and true in spirit.

May you always nurture your inner garden with love and truth, so that the blessings of the Divine continually enrich your life.

Chapter 13

DIVINE PROTECTION

ivine protection is not a mere shield against physical harm, but a profound, spiritual safeguard that transcends the limitations of the material world. It is a cosmic force, an ever-present energy that

surrounds, guides, and nurtures us, whether we are conscious of it or not. Like an invisible force field, divine protection works quietly and steadfastly, ensuring that our souls are always in alignment with higher truth, even amidst the turbulence of life.

In every moment, there is divine intervention that prevents us from harm in ways we cannot always see. Sometimes, we may experience setbacks, challenges, or difficulties, and while they may seem like obstacles, they can be understood as part of a larger divine plan. Every hardship is an opportunity for growth, an invitation to learn deeper lessons, and a sign that the universe is guiding us toward our higher purpose. In such times, divine protection is not the absence of struggle, but the presence of strength and wisdom to navigate through it with grace.

Divine protection also manifests through the presence of spiritual guides, angels, or beings of light who watch over us, offering comfort, direction, and wisdom. They help us stay on course, reminding us of our innate worth and purpose. This protection is not always a visible presence, but it is felt deeply, often as an inner knowing or quiet assurance that we are not alone. It reassures us that no matter how uncertain or difficult life may seem, there is always a higher power holding us in the palm of its hand.

From a spiritual perspective, divine protection works in harmony with our free will. While we are always free to make our choices, there is an underlying divine intelligence that provides us with guidance, whether we are aware of it or not. It offers us signs, synchronicities, and opportunities to align with our true self and to move closer to our ultimate purpose. The more we align ourselves with love, compassion, and truth, the more we invoke this divine protection, allowing it to flow freely into our lives.

Ultimately, divine protection is a reminder that we are part of a larger, sacred design, and we are always held in the embrace of universal love. By trusting in this protection, we learn to surrender our fears and worries, knowing that we are supported by an infinite source of light and grace. This realization brings peace, clarity, and confidence in the unfolding of our journey, no matter the challenges we may face.

———•———

Swamy, you once explained that all human beings carry a spiritual ledger of their deeds, and in that context, you assured us of divine support on our journey. I would like you to also confirm: **"I will protect you from all calamities of life and help you fulfil your mission on earth with majesty and humility."** Please explain the deeper meaning of this promise and how I may understand and embody this assurance in my own journey.

Swamy's Spirit Speaks

Child, the spiritual ledger of your life is a record of every action, thought, and intention, maintained by the immutable law of karma. Yet, amidst the fluctuations of this cosmic account, divine grace continuously flows, ensuring that you are never abandoned. Know this:

- **Divine Protection**

    When I say, *"I will protect you from all calamities of life,"* I do not promise a life free from challenges—challenges are the very catalysts of growth. Rather, I assure you that no matter the obstacles that arise, you will be cradled by the infinite love of the Divine.

    - ✓ This protection is the inner strength that emerges when you cultivate mindfulness and align your actions with truth.

    - ✓ It is the subtle force that turns every setback into a stepping stone, ensuring that even in the darkest moments, you are guided by an unerring light.

- **Fulfilling Your Mission with Majesty and Humility**

    Your unique mission on earth is the purpose for which your soul has journeyed. To fulfil it:

- ✓ **Majesty** reflects the brilliance of your inner light—the honor, passion, and creative power you unleash when you live in harmony with divine principles.

- ✓ **Humility** is the gentle grace that tempers that power. It is the realization that while you are a magnificent expression of the divine, your strength is meant for service rather than self-aggrandizement.

- ✓ Together, these qualities ensure that your journey is not one of mere survival or accumulation, but of graceful transformation and radiant contribution to the world.

◄ **Embodying the Promise:**

To understand and embody this divine promise, you must:

- ✓ **Cultivate Inner Awareness:** Regularly reflect through meditation and mindful practices so that you may perceive the guidance of the divine even amidst life's turbulence.

- ✓ **Act with Integrity:** Align your actions with your highest values. Let every deed, however small, be an offering that honours both the divine and your fellow beings.

- ✓ **Embrace Life's Cycles:** Recognize that every challenge is an invitation for growth. With each trial, trust that divine protection is transforming your inner ledger, turning even hardships into blessings.

- ✓ **Surrender to the Divine Flow:** When your will merges with the divine will, you become an instrument of grace. In that state, the boundaries between effort and divine help dissolve, and you naturally fulfil your mission.

Child, the assurance of protection and guided mission is not a remote promise but a living reality for those who walk the spiritual path with sincerity. Trust that, as you nurture your inner light and act with both majesty and humility, you will be shielded from life's calamities and empowered to fulfil your destiny.

May you always rest in the grace of the Divine, and may your journey on earth be blessed with both strength and gentle humility.

Chapter 14

DIVINE RHYTHM

*D*ivine rhythm is the natural flow of life, an unseen beat that guides the unfolding of existence with grace and purpose. Just as

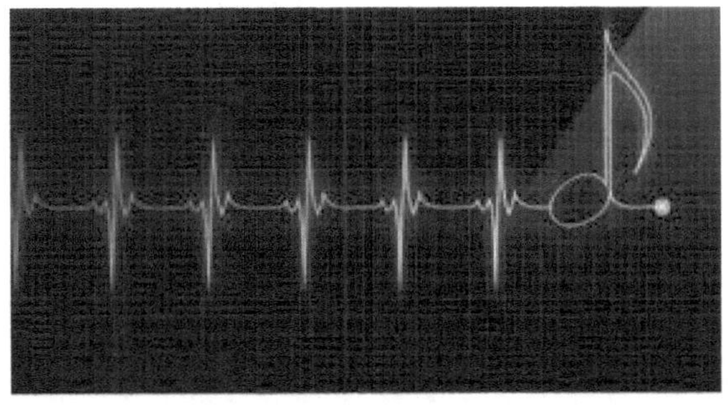

music follows a pattern, with moments of stillness and movement, the universe operates in a rhythm that aligns every part of creation. Each heart that beats, every breath we take, and each change in nature follows a divine cadence, an eternal dance of harmony.

At times, we may feel out of sync with this rhythm, as if our lives are offbeat or chaotic. Yet, even in moments of disarray, divine rhythm continues to flow uninterrupted, reminding us that the ebb and flow of life is part of a greater design. Challenges, joy, sorrow, and growth all occur within this rhythm, and each moment carries its own unique purpose in the cosmic dance. To be in tune with this rhythm is to surrender to life as it unfolds, trusting that each phase, whether still or dynamic, is an essential part of our spiritual journey.

When we align ourselves with the divine rhythm, we experience a deep sense of peace and fulfilment. Like a dancer who surrenders to the music, we move through life with grace, flowing through challenges with resilience and embracing the beauty of each moment. This rhythm teaches us patience and understanding, for we learn that every experience—no matter how small or large—plays a part in the grand symphony of the universe.

In spiritual practice, divine rhythm is often experienced through meditation, prayer, or quiet reflection. It is the stillness in the breath, the awareness of each passing moment, and the realization that we are all connected to a greater universal flow. When we listen deeply, we hear the heartbeat of the cosmos within us, guiding us to our true purpose. As we become more attuned to this rhythm, we release resistance and find our way back to our inner peace, trusting that life's flow will carry us toward greater wisdom and understanding.

Divine rhythm is a reminder that we are not separate from the universe, but an integral part of it. By surrendering to this rhythm, we allow ourselves to be guided by divine intelligence, leading us toward love, compassion, and fulfilment. It is a reminder that in every moment, we are part of something far greater, and our lives are an expression of the divine melody that connects all things.

Swamy, you once said,

"Time is God, Time is Energy, and Track your Time."

While I understand that time is precious, I would like you to explain the deeper essence behind these words with examples so that I may know how to apply this wisdom in my life.

Swamy's Spirit Speaks

Child, these words are a reminder that time is not merely a measurement or a sequence of moments—it is a living, sacred force that shapes your entire existence. Allow me to reveal the essence of each phrase:

- **"Time is God"**
  - ✓ This tells you that time itself is a manifestation of the Divine.
  - ✓ Consider the sunrise: each morning, as the sky lightens, you witness a new beginning—a daily miracle that reminds you that the Divine is always renewing creation.
  - ✓ By seeing time as God, you recognize that every moment holds sacred potential. When you honor each moment, you honor the eternal presence that flows through all things.

- **"Time is Energy"**
  - ✓ Time is the medium through which all energy is expressed.
  - ✓ Just as a battery stores energy to power a device, the moments of your life are filled with potential energy.
  - ✓ For example, when you spend your time in meditation, learning, or serving others, you are channelling this energy into acts that uplift your spirit and transform your life.
  - ✓ Conversely, wasting time on trivial pursuits drains this energy. Thus, your choices determine whether your inner energy is renewed or depleted.

- ◄ **"Track your Time"**
  - ✓ To track your time is to become mindful of how you invest this precious resource.
  - ✓ Imagine an artist who carefully plans each day to create a masterpiece—their schedule ensures that every stroke of effort contributes to the final work.
  - ✓ Similarly, by observing how you spend your moments—be it through work, relationships, or quiet reflection—you gain the wisdom to allocate your time in ways that align with your higher purpose.
  - ✓ This mindfulness helps you avoid distractions and ensures that your actions nourish your growth and well-being.

The Inner Essence

Child, when you embrace these teachings, you learn to see time as a divine, energetic force that you must honor, manage, and invest wisely.

- ◄ **Seeing time as God** transforms how you view every moment—each second becomes an opportunity for renewal and divine connection.
- ◄ **Recognizing time as energy** reminds you that your actions matter, and every moment spent in positive pursuits builds the strength and clarity of your inner being.
- ◄ **Tracking your time** is the practical step of cultivating mindfulness, ensuring that you remain aligned with the eternal flow and do not let life's precious moments slip away in triviality.

In this way, your life becomes a masterpiece—a harmonious blend of sacred moments and conscious actions. May you always be aware of the divine rhythm of time, harness its energy for your growth, and use it to create a life filled with purpose, peace, and profound joy.

Chapter 15

DHARMIC BLISS

Dharmic Bliss is the serene state that arises when we align ourselves with our true purpose in life—the path of Dharma. Dharma is the cosmic law

of righteousness, truth, and duty, guiding us to live with integrity, compassion, and balance. When we walk this path, free from distractions and ego, we experience a profound sense of peace and fulfilment.

In the pursuit of Dharma, we find our deepest joy, not in external rewards but in the alignment of our actions with our higher values. Dharmic Bliss is not fleeting; it's a deep, lasting contentment that comes from knowing we are contributing to the greater good and living authentically. It's a reminder that true happiness arises from living in harmony with ourselves, others, and the universe.

This bliss is cultivated through self-awareness, mindful actions, and an open heart. By embracing Dharmic principles, we transcend the temporary pleasures of life and tap into a source of unshakable peace. Dharmic Bliss teaches us that real joy comes from living truthfully, harmoniously, and in service to something greater than ourselves.

Swamy, you always speak of Sanathana Dharma in simple, profound ways, and you once said,

"Dharmic life is a tasteful life."

Today, this phrase is often used as a catchy slogan, yet many fail to grasp its true meaning. Could you kindly explain, in your eye-opening way, the deeper essence of this statement so that we may understand what it truly means to live a Dharmic life?

Swamy's Spirit Speaks

Child, a Dharmic life is not about adhering to a set of rigid rituals or fashionable trends; it is about embracing life with the full spectrum of divine qualities—much like savoring a rich, intricate flavor that awakens every sense.

◁ A Tasteful Life Defined

- ✓ To say that "Dharmic life is a tasteful life" means that living in accordance with Sanathana Dharma brings out the subtle, nourishing, and refined qualities of existence.
- ✓ Just as a fine meal is prepared with balance, care, and the right ingredients, a life lived with dharma is balanced and imbued with authenticity, compassion, and truth.

◁ The Ingredients of a Dharmic Life

✓ Simplicity and Purity

Living simply allows you to focus on what is truly important—your inner growth, relationships, and the cultivation of virtues.

✓ Discrimination (Viveka)

Like a connoisseur distinguishing between flavors, a Dharmic life involves discerning between what nourishes your soul and what merely distracts or diminishes it.

✓ Compassion and Service (Seva)

True taste comes from sharing—just as the flavor of a dish is enhanced when enjoyed with others, your life gains richness when you serve and uplift those around you.

✓ Steadfastness and Resilience

A tasteful life is not swayed by the transient allure of materialism. It remains rooted in eternal values, even amidst the chaos of the modern world.

◁ The Deeper Essence

✓ Awakening the Inner Palate

When you live a Dharmic life, you develop a sensitive inner palate that discerns the fine nuances of truth and beauty in every experience.

✓ A Life of Harmony

Just as the perfect balance of sweet, sour, salty, and bitter creates a memorable meal, balancing your thoughts, emotions, and actions in accordance with dharma brings you inner peace and fulfilment.

✓ **Transcending Superficiality**

In today's world, the term "dharma" is often reduced to a catchphrase, losing its depth. Yet, a truly Dharmic life is about living with awareness, integrity, and an open heart—a life where every action and every moment resonates with the eternal flavors of love, truth, and beauty.

Child, may you always strive to refine your inner tastes, so that every moment of your life becomes a celebration of the divine essence that dwells within and around you. Embrace simplicity, cultivate discernment, and serve with compassion, and you will find that your life not only becomes tasteful but also deeply meaningful and eternally nourishing.

May the eternal flavors of Sanathana Dharma guide you to live a life that is as rich, balanced, and satisfying as the most exquisite feast.

Chapter 16

SANATHANA DHARMA: A WAY OF LIFE

Sanathana Dharma is not just a set of beliefs; it's a way of living in harmony with the universe. Rooted in timeless wisdom, it teaches us to live with

righteousness, compassion, and self-awareness. Emphasizing values like truth, non-violence, and humility it encourages us to seek balance in all aspects of life—mind, body, and spirit.

Rather than being a rigid doctrine, Sanathana Dharma is a guide for personal growth and spiritual evolution. It invites us to live authentically, respecting all beings, and cultivating inner peace. Through its teachings, we realize that the divine exists in every moment, every action, and every interaction, making every part of life sacred.

Swamy, you beautifully explain Sanathana Dharma and once said,

"It is not to be considered as a religion, but as a way of life that allows self-purification and self-realization."

This is undoubtedly true, but how can it be a way of life from the perspective of common people or even atheists who do not believe in God? How does it detoxify the self and contribute to self-realization? Please illuminate this with your wisdom.

Swamy's Spirit Speaks

Child, Sanathana Dharma is not about belief; it is about **being**. It is not confined to worship or rituals but is a **universal way of living in harmony with oneself, others, and nature.** Whether one believes in a deity or not, the essence of Dharma is about self-elevation, awareness, and inner purification.

Let me explain how Sanathana Dharma serves as a **way of life** and not just a religion:

- **Dharma Is Beyond Religion**
  - ✓ Sanathana Dharma means **eternal principles** that govern existence.
  - ✓ It is not about imposing faith but about **aligning one's thoughts, words, and actions** with truth, justice, and righteousness.
  - ✓ Even an **atheist who follows honesty, compassion, and self-discipline is unknowingly living the principles of Dharma.**

- **Detoxification of the Self**
  Sanathana Dharma purifies the self through:

- ✓ **Sathya (Truth):** Living truthfully removes inner conflicts and guilt.

- ✓ **Ahimsa (Non-violence):** Avoiding harm to others ensures inner peace.

- ✓ **Shaucham (Purity):** Purity of mind, speech, and body leads to clarity.

- ✓ **Santosh (Contentment):** Detachment from greed eliminates stress and anxiety.

- ✓ **Dhyana (Meditation):** Whether through prayer or mindfulness, it helps in detoxifying negative thoughts and emotions.

Self-Realization Without God

For those who do not believe in God, Sanathana Dharma still offers a **path to self-realization** through:

- ✓ **Self-Inquiry:** "Who am I beyond my body, my emotions, my identity?"

- ✓ **Karma Yoga:** Performing actions selflessly without attachment to the outcome.

- ✓ **Jnana Yoga:** Seeking wisdom through reason, logic, and self-reflection.

- ✓ **Inner Balance:** Living in alignment with natural principles brings inner fulfilment.

Dharma in Daily Life for All

- ✓ **A family person** lives Dharma by fulfilling responsibilities with love and sincerity.

- ✓ **A professional** follows Dharma by working ethically and treating colleagues with respect.

- ✓ **A student** practices Dharma by seeking knowledge with humility.
- ✓ **An atheist** upholds Dharma by being truthful, kind, and responsible.

Final Wisdom

Dharma is not about **"whom" you worship but "how" you live.** Whether one prays to a divine force or follows reason alone, the path of Dharma purifies the mind, dissolves ignorance, and reveals the truth about oneself. Self-realization is not about **finding God outside, but discovering the boundless potential within.**

Child, let Dharma guide you, cleanse you, and awaken you—no matter what you believe. The river does not ask whether you believe in water; it simply **flows**—and in that flow, it nourishes all. Be like the river.

Chapter 17

THE DIVINE EMBRACE

In life, we often find ourselves worrying about what lies ahead, trying to control every outcome, and seeking security in a world that feels uncertain. But when we trust in the divine, we release the burden of control and surrender to the understanding that God takes care of everything.

God's care is like a steady current that carries us through life's challenges. It's the silent assurance that, no matter the storm or struggle, we are never alone. Trusting that God takes care doesn't mean we sit idly by; it means we do our best and trust that the divine will guide us, providing what we need at the right time. It is faith in action.

When we embrace this truth, we open our hearts to peace, knowing that the universe has a plan far beyond our understanding. God takes care of our journey—leading, nurturing, and protecting us every step of the way. Let go of fear and trust, for God's care is always present.

Swamy, when I am in the depths of depression, I recall your soothing words:

"He is there, He will take care, always remember God, Namaskaram is the highest, mind gets diverted directly."

While I know this truth, I find it extremely difficult to cope with pressures that exceed my threshold. Could you please explain the deeper essence of these words and guide me on how to truly apply them during such challenging times?

Swamy's Spirit Speaks

Child, these words are a gentle beacon in moments when the weight of depression and overwhelming pressure seems unbearable. Let me share the inner meaning and practical guidance embedded in them:

- **"He is there, He will take care"**
  - ✓ This is a reminder that the Divine presence is always with you, even when you feel isolated or abandoned by the world.
  - ✓ In times of despair, anchor your heart in the knowledge that a loving, protective force—beyond the fluctuations of your emotions—stands ready to support and guide you.
  - ✓ Trusting in this care means relinquishing the burden of trying to control every aspect of your suffering and allowing divine grace to ease your pain.

- **"Always remember God"**
  - ✓ Constant remembrance of God, through prayer or meditation, creates a space of refuge in your heart.

- ✓ When your mind is clouded by darkness, this remembrance acts like a light that cuts through the gloom, reminding you of the eternal truth that you are not alone.

- ✓ It is not about intellectual understanding alone; it is about feeling the Divine presence in every moment, letting it permeate your thoughts and emotions.

◄ **"Namaskaram is the highest"**

- ✓ Namaskaram, or the act of respectful salutation, is a practice of surrender and gratitude.

- ✓ By offering Namaskaram, you acknowledge the Divine in yourself and in every being.

- ✓ This simple act shifts your focus from your personal suffering to the larger, sacred presence that exists in all life.

- ✓ It is a way of expressing humility and opening your heart to receive healing and strength.

◄ **"Mind gets diverted directly"**

- ✓ In times of intense pressure, the mind tends to spiral into negative thoughts and worries.

- ✓ When you engage in practices such as remembrance of God or Namaskaram, your attention is gently diverted from the cycle of distress.

- ✓ This diversion is not about escaping your problems, but about creating a mental space where you can experience peace and clarity—a sanctuary from which healing can begin.

Practical Application

- ◁ **Establish a Daily Practice**

  Dedicate a few moments each day—even in the midst of turmoil—to quietly remember God. It may be through silent meditation, chanting, or simply closing your eyes and feeling the Divine presence.

- ◁ **Use Namaskaram as a Ritual**

  Whenever the weight of depression feels too heavy, pause and offer a humble Namaskaram. Let it be a reminder of the connection you have with something far greater than your temporary pain.

- ◁ **Trust and Surrender**

  Cultivate the inner attitude of trust—that "He is there, He will take care." Allow yourself to surrender your fears and burdens to the Divine, knowing that this act of trust can gradually lighten your load.

- ◁ **Small Steps of Remembrance**

  Even if it feels difficult, try to engage in small acts of remembrance throughout the day. Over time, these practices accumulate, creating a resilient inner space that sustains you during the hardest times.

Child, remember that the journey through darkness is not one of endless suffering but of gradual transformation. The Divine is ever-present, offering a light that, when embraced, guides you to a place of inner peace and renewal.

May you find strength in the certainty that you are never alone, and may these practices help you navigate the stormy seas of life with grace, resilience, and ultimately, profound healing.

HARMONY IN LIFE

Integrating Spiritual Values into
Daily Existence to Cultivate Peace and Fulfilment

Chapter 18

KNOWLEDGE SHOUTS, WISDOM WHISPERS

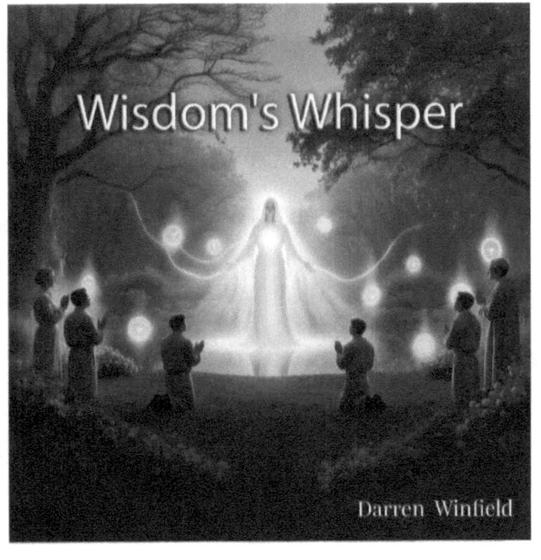

Knowledge is loud, eager to display its depth, to debate, to prove its worth. It fills the mind with facts, figures, and arguments, feeding the ego with a sense of superiority. But wisdom is different—it does not seek attention, nor does it demand validation. It moves in silence, speaking through the stillness of a knowing glance, the simplicity of a kind word, the serenity of presence. The knowledgeable mind seeks to win; the wise heart seeks to understand. Where knowledge divides, wisdom unites. Where knowledge is restless, wisdom is at peace. In the quiet embrace of the Cosmic Mother's grace, wisdom dawns—not in the noise of intellect, but in the stillness of the soul.

Swamy, people often mistake knowledge for wisdom. Filling the brain with facts, figures, and endless information or mastering the art of argument and confrontation—these are all mere extensions of the ego. The knowledgeable mind seeks to win, to prove, to assert. But the wise soul has nothing to prove. Wisdom does not argue; it does not confront. It flows through silence, where words are few but carry the weight of lifetimes. A single glance dissolves doubts, a simple gesture shows the way, and silence itself becomes the voice of truth.

When will I gain such wisdom? Is it not only through the grace of the Cosmic Mother that this becomes possible? True wisdom is not learned; it is received. It is not gathered; it is bestowed. In surrender, in devotion, in silent communion with her, wisdom dawns—not as knowledge, but as light.

The Spirit of Swamy Answers

"You ask, my dear child, but remember—wisdom is not in complexity but in simplicity. Every word you speak, every action you perform, flows not from you but from Her—the Cosmic Mother. She is the doer, the guide, and the giver. You, too, are Her instrument, playing your role, though you may not always understand it in the moment.

When you feel lost in confusion, it is not the world that is unclear, but your mind that wavers. Sit in silence. Do not chase answers, but let them arise within you. In stillness, you will see— everything is interconnected. The flow that moves through you is not your own; it is the Cosmic Mother working through you, guiding your every step.

You fear ignorance, but is it not the burden of knowledge that weighs down the soul? Knowledge shouts, seeking to conquer, to claim, to prove. Wisdom whispers, needing no validation, for it knows that true understanding lies in surrender. The moment you grasp at knowing, you separate yourself from the Divine, and knowledge becomes a cage. Freedom is in dissolving, in unlearning, in allowing Her grace to move you beyond the limits of the mind.

Life is not a puzzle to be solved, but a sacred play to be lived. Sweet and bitter, joy and sorrow—all are threads in Her grand design. You are not the doer, but the witness—detached, yet deeply involved. Act with love, with surrender, and let Her presence flow through you.

And so, my child, you ask—who is the owner, the doer? The answer is Her. She alone owns. She alone acts. You are but a vessel, a channel, a wave in Her vast ocean. When you realize this, you will no longer seek peace—you will become it."

Chapter 19

THE WISDOM OF SELFLESS ACTION

*T*rue wisdom lies in acting without attachment to the fruits of one's actions. The greatest deeds are often those done in silence, without expectation, without seeking  recognition. Just as a river flows without claiming ownership of the life it nurtures, selfless action arises from a pure heart, untouched by the desire for reward.

When we perform our duties with sincerity and love, leaving the results to the Divine, we transcend the burdens of success and failure. Attachment binds, but selflessness liberates. The ego seeks validation, but wisdom understands that the impact of a good deed is not diminished by the absence of acknowledgement.

To act selflessly is to align with the rhythm of the cosmos. A tree does not count the fruits it gives, nor does the sun ask for gratitude for its *light. Likewise, when we give and forget, serve and surrender, we rise above the fleeting illusions of gain and loss, discovering the boundless joy of simply being an instrument of the Divine.*

Swamy, you beautifully said

"Millions of trees in the world are accidentally planted by squirrels, who bury nuts and then forget where they hid them. Do good and forget."

Although I understand the essence of this, I seek your wisdom. How do you perceive this truth? What deeper message do you wish to convey to me?

Swamy's Spirit Speaks

Child, let me explain this beautiful metaphor by drawing upon the wisdom of nature:

- **The Squirrel's Act**
  - ✓ Squirrels bury nuts to store food for later. They do so instinctively, without a conscious plan to create a forest. In their simple, selfless act, they often forget the location of these hidden treasures.
  - ✓ Remarkably, many of these forgotten nuts eventually sprout into trees, enriching the earth and providing shelter and nourishment to countless beings.

- **"Do Good and Forget"**
  - ✓ The essence of my words is to inspire you to perform good deeds without clinging to them or seeking recognition.

- ✓ Just as the squirrel does not boast about its nut-burying, you too should act selflessly, allowing the natural ripple effect of your good actions to flourish on its own.

- ✓ When you do good and then let it go—without attachment—you free yourself from the burden of ego, and your kindness multiplies, creating blessings far beyond what you might imagine.

◄ The Lesson in Nature

- ✓ Nature, in its infinite wisdom, shows us that the most profound contributions often come from acts done purely, without the need for acknowledgement.

- ✓ This teaches you that **true service is its own reward**—it transforms both you and the world, even if you never directly witness the full impact of your actions.

◄ Practical Application

- ✓ In your daily life, strive to act with pure intentions. Whether it's a kind word, a helping hand, or a small gesture of compassion, let these deeds be offered freely.

- ✓ Do not linger on the praise or reward; trust that, like the forgotten nuts that become trees, your acts of kindness will yield bountiful, lasting benefits over time.

Child, the message is simple yet profound: **Live selflessly and let your good deeds be their own reward.** In doing so, you not only lighten your own burden but also sow the seeds of love and growth in the world around you.

May you always be inspired to do good, and may your actions blossom into an abundant legacy that nourishes all life.

Chapter 20

CLEAR MIND, CLEAR LIFE

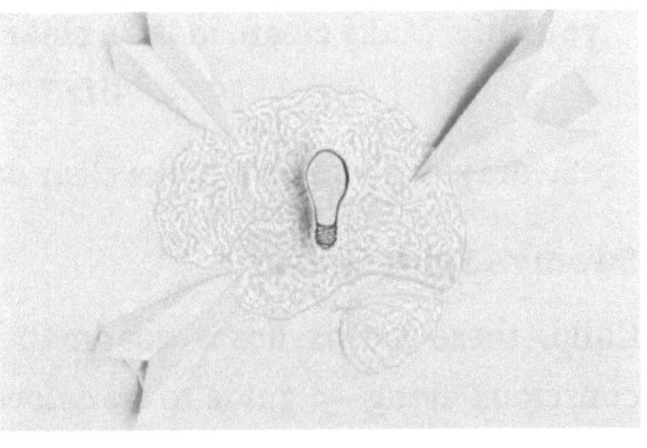

A cluttered mind is like a room filled with unnecessary things—messy, chaotic, and hard to navigate. When thoughts pile up—worries about the future, regrets from the past, and constant comparisons—life feels overwhelming. But when the mind is clear, everything becomes simple and light. Decisions feel natural, relationships become more meaningful, and even the smallest moments bring deep joy.

A calm mind is like a still lake, reflecting life as it is, without distortion. It allows us to see the truth, make wise choices, and respond rather than react. Clarity does not mean having all the answers; it means removing the noise that clouds our thinking. It is not about controlling everything but about letting go of unnecessary burdens and allowing life to unfold naturally.

The more we clear our minds—by releasing negativity, practicing gratitude, and staying present—the more peaceful, purposeful, and joyful our lives become. A clear mind is the key to a clear life, where every step feels lighter, every moment feels meaningful, and inner peace becomes our natural state.

Swamy, you often instruct me to write down,

"Make clear, you will be made clear. Mint your life, maintain your life. Make clean, make a clear mind, and maintain your life."

Swamy, can you now make clear what you truly mean by this?

Swamy's Spirit Speaks

Child, these words are a roadmap for inner purification and conscious living—a guide to transforming not only your external actions but also the very fabric of your inner being. Let me explain their deeper essence:

- **"Make clear, you will be made clear"**
  - **Make clear** means to purify and clarify your thoughts, emotions, and intentions.
  - When you remove the clutter of negativity, doubt, and illusion from your mind, you create a space for true understanding to arise.
  - As your inner vision becomes clearer, the reflection of your true self shines forth, and you, in turn, become clear—both to yourself and to the world.

- ❮ **"Mint your life, maintain your life"**
  - ✓ To **mint your life** is to consciously shape it with intention and creativity, much like minting coins with care and precision.
  - ✓ It means designing your life in alignment with higher principles—cultivating virtues, pursuing meaningful work, and nurturing relationships with sincerity.
  - ✓ **Maintain your life** then calls for constant care and discipline. Once you have created a life that reflects your true values, you must nurture it continuously so that the clarity and beauty you have cultivated do not fade away.
- ❮ **"Make clean, make a clear mind, and maintain your life":**
  - ✓ **Make clean** signifies the cleansing of both your physical surroundings and your inner environment.
  - ✓ A clear mind is one that is free from distracting thoughts, unresolved emotions, and the residue of past errors.
  - ✓ Maintaining your life involves a commitment to ongoing self-reflection and purification, ensuring that you remain aligned with your inner truth.

The Deeper Message

Child, these instructions are not mere guidelines for daily tasks; they are a call to cultivate a state of being where every aspect of your life is infused with clarity, purpose, and inner peace.

- ❮ **By clearing your mind,** you allow the pure light of truth to shine, dispelling illusions and fostering self-awareness.
- ❮ **By minting your life,** you actively create a reality that reflects your highest ideals—turning every action into a meaningful expression of your inner self.

◅ **By maintaining and keeping your inner and outer environments clean,** you set the stage for continuous growth and spiritual evolution.

When you practice these principles, you transform your life into a harmonious blend of action and reflection. In doing so, you not only evolve as an individual but also inspire others to seek their own inner clarity.

May you always have the strength to clear away what no longer serves you, the wisdom to shape your life with intent, and the grace to maintain that purity so that your true self can shine brightly in all you do.

Chapter 21

MINDFUL MASTERY

The mind is a powerful force—it can be our greatest ally or our worst enemy. Most of the time, it wanders aimlessly, trapped in regrets of the past or anxieties about the future. In this endless chatter, we lose touch with the present, where true life unfolds. Psychologically, an untrained mind is reactive, impulsive, and easily disturbed. Spiritually, it is like a wild river—rushing, restless, and untamed.

Mindful mastery is not about controlling the mind forcefully; it is about understanding it, guiding it, and aligning it with purpose. When we become aware of our thoughts, we stop being their prisoners. We begin to respond instead of react, to observe instead of obsessing. The key to mastery is presence—the ability to be fully engaged in the now without distraction. The more we cultivate this awareness, the more we gain clarity, peace, and strength. A mastered mind does not wander—it creates. It does not consume—it elevates. And when we achieve this, life is no longer a struggle—it becomes a flowing harmony of wisdom and action.

Swamy, I observed you saying, "If you put your mind in order, you regain. What do you regain? Good and bad. Reject the bad, entertain the good." This statement intrigued me. Could you kindly explain it with examples to help me grasp its deeper meaning?

Swamy's Spirit Speaks

Your mind is like a vast field, where thoughts grow like seeds. If left unchecked, weeds (negative thoughts) will overrun the good crops (positive thoughts). But when you put your mind in order, you regain clarity—and in that clarity, both good and bad thoughts resurface.

Now comes your responsibility: What will you keep? What will you reject?

- If anger arises, ask yourself—"Does this serve me? Does it bring peace?" If not, reject it.

- If kindness arises, see its power—it softens hearts, builds trust, and brings joy. Entertain it.

- If doubt creeps in, question—"Is it helping me grow, or is it holding me back?" If it weakens your spirit, discard it.

- If faith shines through, observe how it strengthens you. Embrace it.

Take a simple example: A vessel filled with muddy water. If you let the dirt settle, you see the clear water above. Now, you have a choice—will you drink the clean water or stir up the dirt again?

Likewise, when your mind is ordered, you regain all that was within you—both clarity and confusion, strength and weakness. But wisdom lies in choosing to entertain only what uplifts you and discarding what drags you down.

Thus, your mind is your temple, your battlefield, your treasure chest. What you store in it determines your life's journey.

Chapter 22

THE ORDER OF MINDFULNESS

A mind in disorder creates a life in turmoil. When thoughts are scattered, emotions unchecked, and impulses uncontrolled, the result is chaos—both within and in the world around us. We long for peace, yet we entertain conflict. We seek clarity, yet we drown in distractions. This inner disorder spills into our relationships, decisions, and actions, shaping a society that mirrors our own confusion.

True order does not come from external control but from inner discipline. When we take charge of our thoughts, filter negativity, and cultivate awareness, the mind becomes a place of clarity and strength. A mind in order is not restless—it is focused. It does not react—it responds. It sees problems but also envisions solutions. Only when there is harmony within can there be harmony outside. Align the mind, and life itself will align.

———◆———

Swamy, you once showed five fingers and explained that **Space is Brahman, Air is Vishnu, Water is Ganapathi, Fire is Surya, and Earth is the Goddess. Although I am a Brahmin without a thread, I find it difficult to explain this profound truth to others clearly**. Could you kindly illuminate it with examples?

Swamy's Spirit Speaks

The **five elements (Pancha Bhutas)** are not mere physical entities; they are the very foundation of existence, inseparable from divine consciousness. Each element represents an aspect of **universal order** and spiritual realization.

- ◄ **Space (Brahman - Thumb)**: Just as space pervades everything, **Brahman is the all-encompassing reality**, beyond boundaries. Without space, nothing exists—so too, without Brahman, nothing has meaning. **Example**: When you speak, your voice travels through space; similarly, all creation vibrates within Brahman.

- ◄ **Air (Vishnu - Index Finger)**: Air is movement, breath, and life—**Vishnu sustains and pervades all**. Without air, life ceases. **Example**: The breath that keeps you alive is invisible, yet without it, the body collapses. Vishnu, too, is unseen yet ever-present.

- ◄ **Water (Ganapathi - Middle Finger)**: Water **purifies, nourishes, and adapts**, just as **Lord Ganapathi removes obstacles and nurtures wisdom. Example:** A river carves its way through mountains, just as Ganapathi clears your path when you surrender to divine flow.

- ◄ **Fire (Surya - Ring Finger)**: Fire **illuminates, transforms, and energizes**, just as **the Sun (Surya) gives life, light,**

and strength. Example: The fire of knowledge burns away ignorance, just as the Sun dispels darkness each morning.

◁ **Earth (Goddess - Little Finger):** The Earth is **stable, nurturing, and patient—qualities of the Divine Mother. Example:** A mother carries her child just as the Earth bears all life with unconditional love.

Thus, these five fingers are not just symbols; they represent **the divine interplay of existence.** Though you may not wear the sacred thread, **the real thread is awareness of these truths woven into your being.**

When you understand this, **you carry the essence of Brahminhood within, beyond rituals, in your wisdom and actions.**

Chapter 23

UNLOCKING MIND'S POTENTIAL

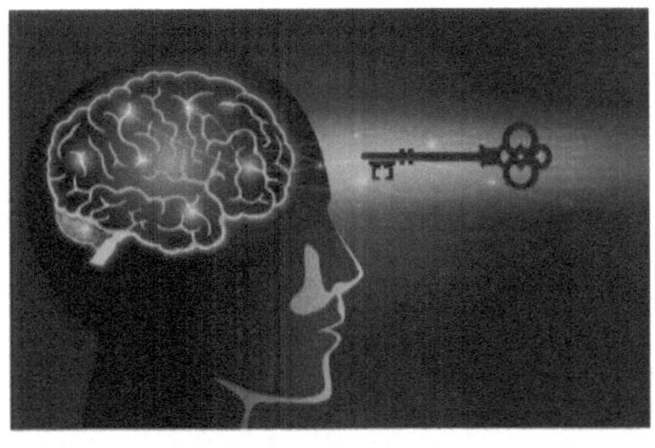

*O*ur mind is a powerful tool, capable of achieving great things, but often we limit its potential by not fully understanding its power. Like a seed that holds the blueprint for a tree, our mind holds the potential for infinite growth, creativity, and transformation. When we learn to quiet the noise of doubt, fear, and distraction, we open the door to the vast wisdom within. By training our mind to focus, to believe, and to trust in its own power, we begin to unlock abilities we never thought possible. The true strength of the mind lies not in controlling everything, but in surrendering to its innate capacity for clarity and insight.

To unlock the mind's potential, we must first free it from the constraints of negativity and self-doubt. Every thought has the power to shape our reality, and when we cultivate positive, focused thinking, we begin to transform our lives. A Sadguru's guidance helps us transcend the limits of the mind, showing us how to tap into deeper wisdom, where true peace and strength reside. Through spiritual *practices, mindfulness, and self-awareness, we can unlock the full potential of our minds—bringing forth a life filled with purpose, joy, and limitless possibility. When we embrace the mind's true power, we realize that we are capable of far more than we ever imagined*

Swamy, you always reiterate that "Mind Energy is Potential Energy." It is true, but how do we tap into it and use it for a good cause? I feel that only God's grace can help in transforming ourselves. Please enlighten me.

Swamy's Spirit Speaks

Child, the mind is like a reservoir—silent, still, yet full of power.

Potential energy lies within you, but real transformation begins when you channel it with awareness.

- Tapping the mind's energy requires three steps

    1. Stillness – A calm mind gathers energy; a restless mind dissipates it.

    2. Direction – Energy without purpose is scattered; focused energy creates transformation.

    3. Application – When energy flows towards goodness, it nurtures, heals, and uplifts.

Understanding the Depth

- A lamp holds potential light, but it must be lit to illuminate.

- A seed holds potential life, but it must be nurtured to grow into a tree.

- Mind energy, when stilled and directed, becomes the force that shapes destiny.

Inner Realization

Child, God's grace is the ignition, but your effort is the wick.

Align your thoughts with dharma, silence the noise within, and allow your mind's potential to become a divine force.

When energy meets awareness, transformation is inevitable. Use it well

Chapter 24

BEYOND THE CHASE

In the rush of life, we often find ourselves chasing after success, wealth, or approval—believing that these things will bring us happiness. But true fulfilment comes not from what we gain but from what we let go of. Beyond the chase lies a state of being where peace, joy, and contentment are not dependent on external achievements but are found within. When we stop constantly running after what we think we need, we make space to appreciate what we already have. It's in this stillness that we realize the treasure was never in the chase, but in the simplicity of being present.

The guidance of a Sadguru helps us move beyond the chase. The Sadguru teaches that real success is not measured by what we collect, but by the peace we cultivate within ourselves. When we detach from worldly desires and focus on our inner growth, we unlock the true essence of life. Beyond the chase, we find the clarity to understand what truly matters—the love we give, the wisdom we share, and the peace we embody. By releasing the endless pursuit and embracing the present moment, we awaken to a life of deep contentment, knowing that we are already whole.

Swamy, you funnily yet intricately shared, "Cat comes, rat comes. The cat wants to catch the rat. Rat should not run away; rat should catch the cat." Although something strikes my mind, I feel you should explain the intention behind this cat-and-rat game.

Swamy's Spirit Speaks

Child, life itself is this game—chasing and being chased.

- The cat represents challenges, fears, and obstacles.
- The rat represents you—your mind, your actions, your responses.

Understanding the Depth:

- If the rat runs away, it remains a prey to fear.
- If the rat turns around and faces the cat, it becomes aware of its own strength.
- Life does not ask you to escape; it asks you to confront.

Inner Realization:

Child, stop running from life's tests.

Turn back, face them, and you will see—sometimes, the cat is more afraid of the rat than the rat is of the cat.

When you stop fearing the chaser, the chaser loses power over you.

Stand your ground, face life, and watch how the game changes.

Chapter 25

BEYOND PERCEPTION

Perception is how we interpret the world around us, shaped by our senses, experiences, and beliefs. Yet, true understanding transcends perception. It's easy to be limited by what we see, hear, or feel in a given moment, but beyond these fleeting impressions lies a deeper truth—one that is not confined to our senses or biases. To go beyond perception is to open the mind to infinite possibilities, to see beyond the surface of things, and to recognize that reality is far greater than our limited viewpoints. When we move beyond perception, we awaken to the timeless and universal truths that bind us all together.

This journey requires letting go of judgments, expectations, and attachments to how things "should" be. It asks us to embrace the unknown, to trust in the unseen, and to allow life to unfold with grace and acceptance. Beyond perception, there is clarity—clarity not born from the mind, but from the soul. It is here that we find true wisdom, free from the distortions of ego and preconceptions.

When we transcend perception, we step into a realm of inner peace and connection, where we no longer define ourselves by external circumstances or appearances. Instead, we simply experience the present moment as it is, with all its beauty, mystery, and truth.

Swamy, on a couple of occasions, you said,

"There are so many masters, unseen, unheard and mystic."

This statement is very intriguing. I want to hear more from you about this, even though I am familiar with the concept of Guru Parampara. Could you please elaborate on what you mean by unseen, unheard, and mystic masters?

Swamy's Spirit Speaks

Child, my words point to a reality beyond the formal lineage of gurus—the Guru Parampara. While you may know the esteemed tradition of recognized masters, understand that true guidance transcends visible form and spoken words. Let me explain:

- **Unseen Masters**
  - There exist countless subtle guides in the realm of inner consciousness.
  - These are the silent energies, the inner voices, and the divine inspirations that help you navigate your path.
  - They do not appear in public or in the conventional sense, yet they are ever-present if you learn to attune your heart.

◄ Unheard Masters

- ✓ Not all masters speak in loud or recognizable tones.
- ✓ Their wisdom comes as a quiet whisper in your mind, or in the gentle prompting of your intuition.
- ✓ When you truly listen, you realize that every moment carries a lesson from the Divine, delivered in silence.

◄ Mystic Masters

- ✓ These are the masters whose presence is felt rather than seen or heard—they are the embodiment of mystery and wonder.
- ✓ They reside in nature, in the arts, in your dreams, and in the depths of meditation.
- ✓ Their teachings are encoded in the very fabric of existence, waiting to be deciphered by a receptive soul.

Child, my intention is to remind you that guidance is not limited to formal teachers or institutions.

◄ True Guidance is Omnipresent

- ✓ Whether it comes from a renowned Guru in a sacred ashram or from the silent whispers of your inner self, all guidance has the same source—the Divine.

◄ Embrace the Subtle

- ✓ Learn to quiet your mind so that the subtle messages from these unseen, unheard, and mystic masters can be discerned.
- ✓ Meditation, deep reflection, and openness to the mysteries of life are your keys to accessing this vast reservoir of wisdom.

◄ **Live with Receptivity**

✓ When you are receptive, every experience becomes a teacher.

✓ The world itself becomes a classroom where even a rustling leaf or a passing cloud speaks of higher truths.

Child, while Guru Parampara is a noble and time-honoured tradition, do not confine your search for wisdom to what is visible or audible. The Divine sends guidance in myriad forms, often in the most unexpected and mystical ways.

May you open your heart and mind to these subtle masters, and may their silent teachings guide you toward the eternal light of truth.

Chapter 26

OBSERVE TO ABSORB

"*Observe to absorb*" is about truly being present in the moment and paying attention to the world around you. It's not just about looking, but about really experiencing life with all your senses. When we take the time to observe, we allow ourselves to absorb wisdom, insights, and lessons from every situation—whether it's from people, nature, or even a quiet moment of reflection.

In a world that moves fast, it's easy to rush through life, missing the small details. But when we slow down and observe with intention, we open ourselves to deeper understanding. We learn not just from what we see or hear, but from how we respond to what's happening around us. This mindful approach helps us grow, teaching us to appreciate life's richness and to discover new perspectives.

By observing thoughtfully, we connect more deeply with ourselves and the world, creating space for wisdom to enter and guide us toward a more fulfilling life.

Swamy, you always said to me,

"Observe to Absorb."

What is the meaning behind these words? How should I understand and internalize their essence? Please explain with kindness.

Swamy's Spirit Speaks

Child, the phrase **"Observe to Absorb"** is an invitation to transform the act of simple observation into a deep, inner process of growth and understanding. Let me share its essence with you:

- **Observation**
  - To observe means to be fully present—attentively witnessing not just the external world, but also your inner thoughts and emotions.
  - This is a mindful practice: you watch without judgment, allowing the details of life, nature, and your own mind to reveal themselves naturally.
  - Through careful observation, you begin to notice patterns, subtle cues, and hidden truths that might otherwise go unnoticed.

- **Absorption**
  - Absorption is the process by which you let what you have observed seep into your inner being.

- ✓ It is more than mere noticing—it is the integration of wisdom, experiences, and lessons into your very essence.
- ✓ As you absorb, you transform external knowledge into internal understanding that nourishes your spirit.

◄ **The Connection**

- ✓ **"Observe to Absorb"** teaches you that every moment is an opportunity for learning and inner evolution.
- ✓ When you observe with a clear, calm mind, you prepare the ground for genuine absorption, where the insights of life enrich your consciousness.
- ✓ This practice leads to a gradual unfolding of inner wisdom, enabling you to respond to life with greater clarity, compassion, and balance.

Child, the beauty of this teaching lies in its simplicity and depth. It is not an intellectual exercise, but a living, breathing practice. By observing mindfully and absorbing deeply, you allow the world to speak to you—transforming everyday experiences into profound lessons on your journey toward truth.

May you always cultivate the art of observation, and may every moment you witness become a stepping stone to a more enlightened and loving life.

Chapter 27

BEYOND MEASURE

In a world where success is often quantified by numbers, achievements, and measurable outcomes, there exists a deeper dimension of life that transcends all forms of measurement. True fulfilment, peace, and love cannot be confined to scales or comparisons; they are boundless, infinite, and immeasurable. To live beyond measure is to embrace the vastness of life in its purest form, where joy, compassion, and wisdom are experienced without the need for validation or applause. It is in this space where we learn to be content with what is, rather than always striving for more.

When we move beyond measure, we release the constraints of societal expectations and personal limitations. We recognize that the essence of life cannot be boxed into accomplishments, wealth, or recognition. Instead, it flourishes in our connection to the present moment, to our own heart, and to the world around us. Living beyond measure is about cultivating an inner peace that remains unaffected by external circumstances. It is about finding value in the intangible—the love we give, the kindness we extend, and the wisdom we share. In doing so, we experience a life that is richer than any measure can quantify, one that is guided by authenticity, grace, and the pursuit of spiritual growth.

Swamy, you simply pass a statement that appears simple at first glance, but when we try to capture its essence, we become lost. What do you mean by,

"Media and Charity is not countable"?

I understand the individual words, yet I sense there is a deeper message here. Is there something specific you wish to communicate to society through this statement? Please explain its inner essence.

Swamy's Spirit Speaks

Child, when I say **"Media and Charity is not countable,"** I invite you to look beyond the surface and understand that the true value of both lies not in numerical measures or material accumulation, but in their qualitative, transformative power. Allow me to explain:

- **Media Beyond Numbers**
  - ✓ **Media** represents all the channels—be it words, art, or technology—through which truth and wisdom are shared.
  - ✓ Its impact is not found in ratings, views, or monetary gains, but in the **depth of transformation** it brings to the heart and mind.
  - ✓ When you use media to communicate divine truths, you engage in a process that transcends quantification; its true worth is felt rather than counted.
- **Charity Beyond Counting**
  - ✓ **Charity** is the act of giving from a place of pure love and selflessness.

- ✓ The real essence of charity is not measured by how much you give, but by the **purity of your intention** and the **spirit in which you serve.**
- ✓ True charity does not keep score—it flows naturally from a heart filled with compassion. Its value is seen in the transformation it inspires, not in the numbers on a ledger.

◅ **The Deeper Message**

- ✓ Both media and charity, when imbued with divine intent, become vehicles for spiritual awakening.
- ✓ They are tools that help dissolve the boundaries between the self and the other, enabling a flow of wisdom and love that cannot be confined to figures or statistics.
- ✓ In this context, "not countable" means that the impact of genuine media and heartfelt charity is immeasurable— it is the quality of life they uplift, the inner light they kindle, and the unity they foster among people.

Child, I urge you to look beyond conventional measures. Understand that the true worth of our expressions and our giving is in the **spiritual transformation** they inspire. When you share with a pure heart, when you communicate with wisdom, you touch lives in ways that numbers can never capture.

May you always strive to express and give in ways that enrich the soul, knowing that the true impact of your actions is infinite and beyond counting.

Chapter 28

MOVING WITH PURPOSE

Moving with purpose means living with intention, knowing why you do what you do. It's about making sure your actions reflect what truly matters to you. Just like a river flows steadily toward the ocean, when we move with purpose, we have a clear direction that guides us through life. It's not about rushing to finish something, but making each moment meaningful as we move forward.

When we live with purpose, we focus on what's important and avoid getting lost in distractions. It helps us stay calm and steady, even when things get tough. Moving with purpose doesn't mean everything will be easy, but it gives us a sense of fulfillment because we know each step is leading us to something meaningful. It's not about success in the eyes of the world, but about living authentically and in line with our true values. When we move with purpose, we create a life full of peace, growth, and the satisfaction that comes from knowing we're following the path meant for us.

Swamy, you once said,

"If one wants to click their life then move like a clock hand."

What is the intention behind this statement? What do you mean by "click their life," and why should one move like a clock hand? Please explain the inner essence of these words in your unique way so that we may understand their deeper significance.

Swamy's Spirit Speaks

Child, this statement is a metaphor for aligning your life with the natural, steady rhythm of the universe. Allow me to reveal its essence:

- **"Click their life"**
  - ✓ To "click" means for your life to fall into place— when every moment, every action, and every decision harmonizes with your inner truth.
  - ✓ It is the state of alignment where your potential, purpose, and passion converge, much like the smooth interlocking of gears in a well-functioning machine.
- **"Move like a clock hand"**
  - ✓ A clock hand moves with unwavering consistency and discipline. It never rushes, yet it never stops; it follows a natural, rhythmic pattern that marks the passage of time.
  - ✓ By moving like a clock hand, you are encouraged to adopt a balanced, persistent pace in life—one that is neither frantic nor stagnant.
  - ✓ This steady movement implies that progress is made through continuous, deliberate actions. Each tick is a

moment to grow, reflect, and advance, however small the step.

◁ The Inner Essence

✓ **Discipline and Consistency:** Just as the clock hand does not waver from its path, your life must be guided by disciplined, consistent actions.

✓ **Harmony with Time:** Recognize that every moment holds the potential for transformation. When you are in tune with the natural rhythm of time, you allow the subtle energies of the universe to work through you, making your life "click" into place.

✓ **Flow and Balance:** The movement of the clock hand is smooth and balanced. Likewise, embrace a lifestyle that fosters inner balance—where your thoughts, emotions, and actions are aligned with your highest values.

Child, the message is not to rush or force outcomes but to move with a natural, steady cadence. As you align yourself with this rhythm, the pieces of your life will gradually interlock, revealing a harmonious pattern of growth and fulfilment.

May you learn to live each moment with mindful discipline and gentle persistence so that your life unfolds with clarity, purpose, and inner joy.

Chapter 29

THE STRENGTH OF INNER CLARITY

ourageous clarity is the strength to see things clearly, even when the path ahead is uncertain. It's about having the bravery to face the truth—whether it's about ourselves, our situations, or the world around us—and the wisdom to take decisive action based on that truth. This clarity doesn't come from having all the answers, but from the courage to embrace what is, and to move forward with confidence, even when we don't know exactly what the future holds.

When we have courageous clarity, we aren't afraid to make tough decisions or face challenges head-on. We trust ourselves to navigate through life's complexities, knowing that our inner vision will guide us through uncertainty. It's about finding the courage to act on what we know to be right, even when it's uncomfortable or difficult. With courageous clarity, we create the space to grow, to learn, and to step into our fullest potential, no matter the obstacles. It's the bravery to see clearly and the strength to move forward with purpose and conviction.

Swamy, your words are always encouraging. You once said,

"Be bold, be brave, and balance your mind."

While I understand the general intention behind these words, I would like you to explain their deeper essence so that I may fully grasp and embody this message.

Swamy's Spirit Speaks

Child, this simple yet powerful statement is a call to transform the way you engage with life on every level—emotionally, mentally, and spiritually. Let me explain each part for you:

- **Be Bold**
  - ✓ To be bold is to step forward with conviction and to trust in your inner vision.
  - ✓ It means not being afraid to pursue your truth or to express your unique self, even in the face of uncertainty.
  - ✓ Boldness is about taking risks with your heart open, embracing opportunities without being paralyzed by fear or doubt.

- **Be Brave**
  - ✓ Bravery is the courage to face life's challenges head-on.
  - ✓ It is the strength to confront adversity, to endure hardships, and to rise each time you fall.
  - ✓ Bravery does not mean the absence of fear; rather, it is the determination to act in spite of it.
  - ✓ When you are brave, you allow your spirit to soar above obstacles, trusting that every challenge is an opportunity for growth.

- **Balance Your Mind**

  - ✓ Balancing your mind involves cultivating equanimity amid the constant flow of thoughts, emotions, and external influences.

  - ✓ It is about finding a state of inner harmony where you are neither overwhelmed by excitement nor weighed down by worry.

  - ✓ A balanced mind is like a calm lake reflecting the sky; it holds the clarity and stillness needed to see the truth of every situation.

  - ✓ This balance supports both bold action and brave endurance by keeping you centred and grounded.

The Inner Essence

Child, when you integrate boldness, bravery, and mental balance, you create a powerful synergy within yourself. This triad of qualities enables you to:

- **Act with Conviction**

  With boldness, you move forward confidently, trusting that your path is guided by inner wisdom.

- **Face Adversity with Courage**

  Bravery empowers you to overcome setbacks and learn from every experience, turning challenges into stepping stones.

- **Maintain Inner Harmony**

  A balanced mind allows you to stay calm and composed, ensuring that your actions remain aligned with your higher purpose, no matter how turbulent the external world may be.

Together, these qualities form a way of living that is both dynamic and stable—a life that is fearless yet grounded, ever-moving yet always centered. In this way, you not only meet life's challenges head-on but also transform them into opportunities for growth and inner evolution.

May you always find the courage to be bold, the strength to be brave, and the wisdom to balance your mind, so that you may live a life that truly reflects your highest self.

Chapter 30

BALANCED BEING

A balanced being is someone who harmonizes the various aspects of their life—physical, mental, emotional, and spiritual—into a unified whole. It is the embodiment of inner peace and outer harmony, where thoughts, actions, and emotions align with the deeper essence of self. A balanced being understands the importance of moderation, not swinging between extremes but cultivating a state of equilibrium that fosters well-being and growth.

True balance is found in the ability to stay grounded in the present moment, while being open to change and adaptation. It's about recognizing the value in both action and stillness, success and failure, joy and sorrow. A balanced being knows that life is a dance of contrasts and learns to flow gracefully through both calm and turbulence. They nurture their body with healthy habits, cultivate a calm and clear mind, and nourish the soul with love and spiritual practice.

From a spiritual perspective, balance is an expression of inner wisdom, where the self is in tune with the universe. It is the recognition that everything in life has its place and purpose. A balanced being seeks unity with all that is, without being swayed by the fleeting distractions of the material world. They understand that peace is not found in external circumstances but within themselves. By embodying balance, they not only find fulfilment and joy but also radiate peace to those around them, creating a ripple effect of harmony.

Swamy, you once said,

"Master outside, Monk inside."

What do you mean by this, and how should I understand its deeper essence?

Swamy's Spirit Speaks

Child, this statement is a profound reminder of the duality required on the spiritual path—an invitation to harmonize the external role of leadership with the inner life of deep renunciation and self-discipline.

◄ Master Outside

- ✓ This refers to the outward expression of wisdom, guidance, and leadership.
- ✓ As a master, you are called to inspire others, teach through your actions, and embody the qualities of strength, clarity, and compassion in the world.
- ✓ Your external demeanor should be that of a confident guide—someone who lights the way for others and whose actions uplift society.

◄ Monk Inside

- ✓ In contrast, the inner life must remain that of a monk—a state of humility, simplicity, and introspection.

- ✓ A monk is one who lives detached from the trappings of ego, remains deeply connected to the inner self, and continuously practices self-discipline and meditation.

- ✓ This inner sanctum of calm and renunciation is where true spiritual transformation occurs.

The Harmonious Balance

- ✓ The beauty of this teaching lies in the balance it encourages: externally, you should fulfil your responsibilities as a teacher or leader, radiating wisdom and positivity; internally, however, you must remain humble and detached, continuously refining your spirit through introspection and surrender.

- ✓ This duality ensures that while you influence the world positively, you never lose sight of your inner journey and the divine essence that underlies all actions.

Why This Matters

- ✓ Many become so absorbed in their external achievements and recognition that they neglect the inner discipline required for true spiritual growth.

- ✓ By maintaining the "Master outside, Monk inside" posture, you serve as a beacon of balanced living—one who inspires others without being corrupted by ego, and who remains rooted in truth despite worldly challenges.

Child, remember that the path to spiritual fulfilment is not just about external accomplishments but about the quality of your inner life. Embrace this dual approach: lead with your outer actions and nurture a silent, devoted inner sanctuary. In this way, you become a true master—both to yourself and to those you guide.

May you always balance the brilliance of your external influence with the serene depth of your inner wisdom.

Chapter 31

FLOWING YET ROOTED

In life, there are moments when we must flow with the currents of change and moments when we need to fix and stabilize what is within our control.

"Flow" is about embracing the natural rhythm of life, allowing ourselves to adapt to circumstances, trusting in the process, and accepting that some things are beyond our immediate influence. It's a state of ease where we allow ourselves to be guided by the present moment, accepting the unpredictability of life with an open heart.

On the other hand, "Fix" speaks to the power of action and responsibility. There are times when we must take charge, repair what is broken, and correct our course. Fixing is about addressing the challenges that arise and making deliberate efforts to restore balance, improve situations, or resolve conflicts. It's not about stubbornly holding onto the past, but about recognizing where change is needed and taking steps to bring about that change.

The art lies in knowing when to flow and when to fix. A wise person understands that both are necessary—sometimes we need to surrender to the flow of life, and at other times, we need to take decisive action to fix what is out of alignment. In the balance of flow and fix, we discover the power of flexibility and the strength of resolve. It is through this understanding that we navigate life's complexities with grace and purpose, achieving harmony in our personal and spiritual journeys.

Swamy, you mentioned once,

"Enough is energy, don't fix and follow, but follow and fix."

Please explain to me how to achieve this state. What does it mean to not fix and follow but instead to follow and fix? I wish to understand its deeper essence so that I may embody this wisdom in my life.

Swamy's Spirit Speaks

Child, these words are a call to embrace the dynamic nature of life and to transform the way you engage with the world. Let me share the inner meaning with you:

- **"Enough is energy"**
  - ✓ This phrase reminds you that the true resource of life is not static wealth or fixed opinions, but the vibrant, ever-present energy that flows within and around you.
  - ✓ When you tap into your inner energy, you discover that there is always enough—enough strength, inspiration, and potential—to overcome obstacles and fuel your growth.

- **"Don't fix and follow"**
  - ✓ To "fix" means to adhere rigidly to a particular idea, method, or system. When you fixate on something, you risk becoming stagnant and blind to the changes around you.
  - ✓ "Follow" without question may lead you to mimic others, losing your individuality and the opportunity to develop your own wisdom.
  - ✓ In other words, if you simply fix and then follow, you allow external patterns to dictate your life without truly understanding or adapting to the flow of energy.

- **"But follow and fix"**
  - ✓ This part of the teaching urges you to first observe the natural currents of life—follow them with an open heart and a receptive mind.
  - ✓ Once you have learned from the dynamic flow of energy around you and within you, then you "fix" or establish your own path, one that is deeply rooted in the truths you have discovered.
  - ✓ It is a process of dynamic learning and then purposeful anchoring; you absorb life's lessons before setting your own, clear direction.

How to Achieve This State

1. Cultivate Awareness

- Practice mindfulness and meditation to become attuned to the flow of energy in every moment.
- Observe your thoughts, emotions, and actions without judgment, allowing you to perceive the natural rhythm of life.

2. **Embrace Flexibility**

   ⊰ Remain open to change. Allow yourself to be guided by the insights that arise from experiencing life fully, rather than clinging to fixed ideas or routines.

   ⊰ Understand that growth comes from adapting and evolving.

3. **Set Purposeful Intentions:**

   ⊰ Once you have absorbed the lessons from life's flow, fix your vision by setting clear, deliberate intentions that align with your inner truth.

   ⊰ Let these intentions guide your actions, providing a stable foundation amid the ever-changing currents of life.

4. **Integrate and Balance:**

   ⊰ Balance the dynamic energy you absorb with a steady inner core. This is the essence of "follow and fix"—learn from the flux and then establish a grounded, purposeful path.

   ⊰ In this balanced state, your actions become both responsive to the moment and aligned with your deepest values.

Child, by following this process, you transform your life from a reactive pattern of simply imitating others into a creative journey of self-realization. You become an active participant in the divine dance, letting the abundant energy of the universe guide you and then anchoring that wisdom in your own unique way.

May you always be in tune with the natural flow of life and have the courage to set your own purposeful course, allowing your inner light to shine brilliantly in all that you do.

MINDFUL SURRENDER

Mindful surrender is the conscious act of releasing control while remaining fully aware of the present moment. It is not about giving up or resigning to passivity, but about embracing life with acceptance and trust. In a world that often encourages forceful effort and relentless striving, mindful surrender invites us to pause, reflect, and allow things to unfold naturally. It's about letting go of attachments to specific outcomes and accepting the flow of life as it comes, without resistance or struggle.

At its core, mindful surrender is about cultivating inner peace by releasing the need to control every aspect of our journey. It encourages us to trust in the larger design of life, knowing that there is wisdom beyond our limited understanding. When we surrender mindfully, we open ourselves to growth, learning, and transformation. It is through this release that we make space for new opportunities and deeper wisdom to emerge.

In spiritual terms, mindful surrender is the key to aligning with the divine will. It is a practice that allows us to merge with the flow of the universe, where we are no longer separate from the greater whole. By surrendering our ego, fears, and desires, we find peace and freedom, recognizing that our true strength lies in trusting the unfolding of life's journey. In surrender, we not only find liberation, but we also connect with a deeper sense of purpose and meaning, leading us closer to the divine essence within and around us.

Swamy, you often tell those who gather around you,

"Don't repeat; request your mind not to think negative, but put forward pure energy thought into heart-soul—that means surrender to soul."

I understand the general idea behind your words, but I struggle to grasp their full depth. Could you please explain the inner essence of this message in your unique way so that my perception—and that of others—may broaden?

Swamy's Spirit Speaks

Child, these words are an invitation to free yourself from the habitual cycles of negativity and to consciously embrace the pure, transformative energy within you. Let me unfold their deeper meaning:

- **"Don't repeat"**
    - ✓ This is a call to break the cycle of repetitive, negative thought patterns and behaviors.

- ✓ Every moment is a new opportunity; do not allow your mind to replay the same unhelpful narratives that keep you trapped in despair or anger.

◄ **"Request your mind not to think negative"**

- ✓ Rather than forcefully suppressing thoughts, gently ask your mind to let go of negativity.

- ✓ This is a compassionate approach, inviting your thoughts to shift from pessimism to a more positive, life-affirming perspective.

◄ **"But put forward pure energy thought into heart-soul"**

- ✓ Here, you are encouraged to actively channel pure, positive energy into your inner being.

- ✓ This means cultivating thoughts that resonate with love, compassion, and wisdom, so that they fill your heart and soul with light.

- ✓ It is the deliberate process of replacing negativity with uplifting ideas, nurturing your inner garden with the seeds of hope and joy.

◄ **"That means surrender to soul"**

- ✓ Ultimately, this is about letting go of the ego and the habitual mind, and allowing your higher self—your soul—to guide you.

- ✓ Surrender, in this context, is not about giving up but about trusting the deeper wisdom that resides within you.

- ✓ When you surrender to your soul, you open yourself to divine grace and inner transformation, transcending the cycle of negative repetition.

Child, by practicing this gentle yet powerful process, you gradually free your mind from the chains of repetitive negativity. You create space for the pure energy of life to flow into your heart, nourishing your soul and guiding you toward inner peace and true clarity.

May you always find the strength to ask your mind for the light of truth, to channel pure energy into your being, and to surrender with humility to the wisdom of your inner soul. In doing so, you align yourself with the divine flow, transforming every moment into an opportunity for growth and joy.

Chapter 33

TRUE WORTH

*T*rue worth is not determined by external measures such as wealth, status, or achievements. It is found in the depth of one's character, the kindness extended to others, and the authenticity with which one lives. In a world that often measures success by material possessions and outward appearances, true worth is rooted in the inner qualities that define a person—compassion, humility, integrity, and resilience.

The essence of true worth lies in the way we treat others, especially when no one is watching. It's about making choices that reflect our values and being true to ourselves, regardless of external expectations. True worth is also about embracing our flaws and imperfections, understanding that our vulnerabilities make us human and help us grow. It's about living with purpose, guided by principles that transcend the superficial and connect us to something greater than ourselves.

In spiritual terms, true worth comes from aligning with the divine essence within. When we connect with our higher self, we realize that our worth is inherent, not earned. It is not dependent on what we accumulate or accomplish but on the love and light we share with the world.

True worth is a reflection of our soul's journey, and it can only be measured by the positive impact we have on the lives of others and the world around us.

Swamy, you once shared,

"Media and charity are not countable parts of your recognition."

Does this mean that there is no need for publicity or external acknowledgment for good deeds and charitable actions? Please explain the deeper essence behind this statement.

Swamy's Spirit Speaks

Child, these words are a reminder that true worth is measured not by numbers or external accolades, but by the purity of your intentions and the transformation within your heart. Let me share the essence of this teaching:

- **Media as a Tool, Not a Measure**
  - **Media** represents all forms of external communication—be it praise, awards, or public recognition.
  - However, the light of your good deeds does not shine based on how many people notice it.

- ✓ True goodness is inherent and self-sustaining; it is not quantified by headlines or numbers, but by its capacity to uplift souls.

- ✓ The focus should be on the integrity of your actions rather than on seeking external validation.

Charity Beyond Countable Metrics

- ✓ **Charity** is the act of giving selflessly, from a heart filled with compassion.

- ✓ Its value is not in how much you give in measurable terms, but in the sincerity with which you give.

- ✓ When you perform acts of charity, the true reward lies in the transformation that occurs—both in the one who gives and the one who receives.

- ✓ It is not the tally of your contributions that matters, but the light you kindle in the world.

Recognition of the Inner Self

- ✓ When you engage in good deeds without the desire for publicity, you cultivate an inner strength and humility that no external honor can bestow.

- ✓ The recognition that truly counts is the one you receive from within—a sense of peace, fulfilment, and alignment with the divine.

- ✓ This inner recognition is everlasting, whereas external validation is fleeting and often fades away with time.

The Ultimate Message

- ✓ I urge you to let go of the need to be seen or counted for your good actions.

- ✓ Instead, focus on nurturing the inherent goodness within you.

- ✓ When you act from a place of genuine compassion and selflessness, you contribute to a higher order of life that transcends the transient measures of society.

- ✓ In this way, media and charity become tools for inner growth rather than the final goals of your journey.

Child, know that the beauty of your actions lies in their authenticity.

May you always strive to act with a pure heart, knowing that the divine reward is the inner light and peace that will always remain with you—beyond any countable measure or public acclaim.

Chapter 34

MIND MASTERY

Mind mastery is the art of controlling your thoughts, emotions, and reactions to navigate life with clarity and purpose. It is the ability to observe your thoughts without becoming overwhelmed by them,  *choosing your responses with intention rather than being swept away by impulsive reactions. This mastery begins with awareness—the realization that you are not your thoughts, but the observer of them.*

When we practice mind mastery, we move beyond automatic reactions and patterns, opening ourselves up to the present moment. This allows us to live with greater peace, focus, and resilience. Mastery of the mind empowers us to make decisions that align with our true values, not our temporary emotions or external pressures. It helps us find balance and harmony, even in challenging situations, as we cultivate a deep sense of inner calm and mental clarity.

On a spiritual level, mind mastery is key to transcending the limitations of the ego and connecting with the divine essence within. By mastering the mind, we free ourselves from negative thought patterns and align more closely with our higher consciousness. It is through this control that we can deepen our awareness, elevate our lives, and contribute positively to the world around us. True mind mastery isn't about suppressing thoughts but learning how to guide and direct them to serve our highest purpose.

And here's a little spiritual humour to lighten the path of mind mastery:

Why did the yogi refuse to use a GPS?

Because he already knows that the journey to inner peace starts within

---

Swamy, you once said,

"Whoever controls their mind will become master."

This is a wonderful statement, yet it raises a challenging question: How can one control the mind? The mind is a bundle of desires—both desirable and undesirable. It lacks discrimination and constantly yearns to own and grasp. Though it may seem almost impossible to achieve such control, please share your wisdom on how one can master the mind and thereby become the true master of one's life.

Swamy's Spirit Speaks

Child, the mind is indeed a turbulent ocean of desires, impulses, and restless thoughts. To master the mind is to transform this chaos into a wellspring of clarity and strength—a journey that requires patience, practice, and divine grace. Let me share the essence of this teaching with you:

- **Understanding the Nature of the Mind**
  - ✓ The mind is like a wild, untamed horse or a rapidly flowing river. It is naturally inclined to roam, to grasp at every passing desire, whether beneficial or harmful.
  - ✓ Its constant urge to own and accumulate comes from the ego, which clouds discrimination and fuels both attachment and aversion.

- **The Process of Mastery**
  - ✓ **Cultivate Awareness**

    Begin by observing your thoughts without judgment. Notice the arising of desires, doubts, and impulses. In this quiet observation, you start to recognize patterns and triggers that disturb your inner peace.

  - ✓ **Practice Mindful Detachment**

    Learn to let go of the need to cling to every thought or desire. Detachment does not mean indifference; rather, it means engaging with life without being enslaved by your impulses.

  - ✓ **Engage in Regular Meditation:**

    Meditation is the tool that tames the restless mind. With consistent practice, you learn to create moments of deep stillness—a space where the turbulent waves of desire settle into a calm, reflective pool.

✓ **Align with Higher Values**

Redirect the mind's energy by consciously cultivating virtues such as compassion, humility, and selflessness. When you focus on higher ideals, the mind gradually learns to discriminate between what nourishes your soul and what merely feeds the ego.

◁ **The Role of Divine Grace**

✓ Understand that while the discipline of the mind is a personal endeavour, it is greatly aided by divine grace.

✓ When you surrender to the higher wisdom within, the divine spark guides you, subtly transforming even the most chaotic thoughts into stepping stones for growth.

✓ It is not solely by your effort, but by aligning your will with the eternal, that true mastery of the mind is achieved.

◁ **The Ultimate Transformation**

✓ As you learn to control and harness the mind's energy, you do not eradicate desires completely; instead, you transform them.

✓ The wild impulses of the mind gradually become channels of creativity and inner strength.

✓ In this state, you become the master—able to navigate life's complexities with calm assurance and deep insight.

Child, mastering the mind is not an overnight achievement but a continuous journey of inner cultivation. Embrace each moment of awareness, practice detachment with compassion, and allow the grace of the Divine to guide you. In time, you will discover that what once seemed impossible becomes the very foundation of your true power and freedom.

May you always be blessed with clarity and strength on this path of inner mastery, and may your mind become a serene instrument of divine truth.

Chapter 35

KARMIC LEDGER

Karmic Ledger is an intriguing concept that can be understood as the spiritual balance we create through our actions, thoughts, and intentions. Just like a bank account, each positive deed or pure thought is deposited into the universal energy ledger, accumulating credit in the form of good karma. These credits aren't tangible or measurable by material means, but they influence our lives in ways that transcend the physical world.

In the grand cosmic scheme, the universe doesn't work on a system of right or wrong; rather, it revolves around the law of cause and effect. Every action, word, and intention we put into the world either adds to our cosmic credit or diminishes it. Positive actions, guided by love, kindness, and compassion, build our cosmic balance, creating opportunities for growth, happiness, and peace. Negative actions, born from greed, hatred, or ignorance, result in a debit, leading to life lessons that help us grow.

Spiritual teachings suggest that the more we focus on generating good credit in the form of selfless service, mindful thoughts, and virtuous actions, the greater the harmony and positivity that flow into our lives. The beauty of cosmic credit is that it operates beyond human perceptions of time and space. Whether you see it or not, every good deed sends ripples through the universe, returning to you in ways that are often unexpected but always timely.

On a deeper level, cosmic credit reflects our connection to the divine and the greater good of the universe. It encourages us to live in alignment with universal truths, knowing that every positive contribution, no matter how small, is recorded in the cosmic ledger. This understanding empowers us to live with intention and purpose, knowing that we are constantly building a life of greater fulfilment and spiritual growth.

In simpler terms: Life is a cosmic game of deposit and withdrawal. Make sure you're filling up that account with kindness, love, and good intentions. The return? Infinite and abundant.

———◆———

Swamy, you once said,

"All human beings are credit card holders."

What do you mean by this statement? What are the concepts of debit and credit in this context, and how does one balance them? What are these accounts, and who maintains them?

Swamy's Spirit Speaks

Child, this metaphor is a way to describe the spiritual ledger that every soul carries—a record of actions and intentions that determines the quality of your life and growth. Let me explain its deeper essence:

- ◄ **The Spiritual Ledger**
  - ✓ Imagine your life as an ongoing account maintained by the universal law of karma.
  - ✓ In this account, every good deed, pure thought, and selfless action acts as a credit, while every negative action, harmful thought, or selfish deed acts as a debit.
  - ✓ Just as in financial terms, the balance of this account influences your overall well-being and future experiences.

- ◄ **Credit and Debit**
  - ✓ **Credit** symbolizes the positive energy and virtues you accumulate. It is the spiritual currency that builds your character and attracts blessings.
  - ✓ **Debit** represents the negative actions and thoughts that drain your inner resources. These are the obstacles and burdens that hinder your progress.
  - ✓ The goal is to maintain a positive balance—a state of being where the credits of kindness, compassion, and truth outweigh the debits of ego, greed, and negativity.

- ◄ **Balancing the Account**
  - ✓ **Awareness and Self-Reflection:** Regularly reflect on your actions and thoughts. Meditation and mindful practices help you recognize what is adding positive value and what is subtracting from your inner wealth.
  - ✓ **Corrective Action:** When you notice debits accumulating, take corrective steps. Repent, learn, and consciously transform negative habits into positive ones.

- ✓ **Consistent Virtue:** Cultivate and practice virtues consistently. Just as a diligent saver maintains a healthy bank account, your consistent efforts in doing good will keep your spiritual balance in check.

- ◄ **Who Maintains the Account:**
  - ✓ This account is maintained by the cosmic law of karma, which is impartial and all-knowing.

  - ✓ It is not managed by any human institution but is overseen by the divine wisdom that recognizes the true intentions behind each action.

  - ✓ Ultimately, you are also the custodian of your own account through your choices and reflections. By being conscious of your deeds, you actively participate in balancing your spiritual ledger.

Child, the metaphor of being "credit card holders" is a reminder that every action matters. The energy you invest in the world—whether positive or negative—determines the future you experience.

- ◄ Strive to make more deposits of goodness than withdrawals of negativity, and you will find that your life flows with greater peace, prosperity, and spiritual fulfilment.

- ◄ Remember, the journey is continuous, and every moment is an opportunity to improve your balance.

May you always be mindful of your spiritual transactions and nurture an abundant inner wealth that guides you toward truth and harmony.

Chapter 36

SELF-DIRECTED PRAYER

Self-directed prayer is a deeply personal and transformative practice that empowers us to connect directly with the divine from the core of our being. Unlike traditional prayers that follow prescribed words or rituals, self-directed prayer is an open channel of communication between the individual soul and the divine presence, shaped by one's thoughts, emotions, and intentions. It is not confined by external structures, but rather flows freely from within, guided by the purity of the heart and the clarity of the mind.

In self-directed prayer, we step into our own inner temple, seeking a direct experience of the divine. This prayer is an expression of our deepest desires, our fears, our gratitude, and our surrender. It invites us to be real with ourselves, stripping away the facades and reaching out to the divine with authenticity. When we pray in this way, we are not merely asking for things but are engaging in a conversation—an intimate exchange of energy and love with the divine, where we both listen and speak.

One of the greatest strengths of self-directed prayer is its flexibility and adaptability. It can happen at any time, in any place, and in any form that resonates with the individual. It might be a silent prayer, a spoken word, or even a prayer through action. It allows us to be fully present in the moment, harnessing the power of our intention to manifest the divine's guidance, grace, and protection. The more we engage in self-directed prayer, the deeper our connection to the divine becomes, nurturing our inner strength and clarity.

At its essence, self-directed prayer is a practice of self-awareness and alignment with the divine. It reminds us that the divine is not distant or separate from us, but is an ever-present force within us. Through this personal prayer, we become attuned to the divine flow within our own hearts and minds, allowing us to align our actions, thoughts, and emotions with the greater purpose of life. In doing so, we discover a profound sense of peace and purpose, knowing that we are always supported by the divine, both in moments of joy and in times of struggle.

In spiritual terms, self-directed prayer is a form of surrender—an act of letting go of our ego and trusting in the divine wisdom that guides us. It is the path of self-realization, where we understand that the true power of prayer lies not in asking, but in being receptive to the divine presence that resides within us and the world around us.

Through self-directed prayer, we become conduits for divine energy, allowing it to flow freely through us and into the world, illuminating our lives and the lives of others.

—•◆•—

Swamy, you once said,

"Prayer is perfect when you pray yourself."

I wonder: does this mean that others cannot pray for me, or that I can pray for others? The statement seems complex to me. Could you simplify and explain the deeper essence of this message?

Swamy's Spirit Speaks

Child, my words are meant to inspire you to cultivate a direct, personal connection with the Divine through prayer. Allow me to clarify:

- **Personal Engagement**
  - ✓ When I say, **"Prayer is perfect when you pray yourself,"** I emphasize that the most transformative prayer is the one that comes from your own heart.
  - ✓ It is through your personal, sincere engagement with the Divine that you awaken the inner light and nurture your soul.
  - ✓ Self-prayer creates an intimate dialogue between you and the Divine, allowing you to understand your own heart and align with higher truth.

- **The Role of Others' Prayers**
  - ✓ This teaching does not mean that the prayers of others are without value. When others pray for you, their good intentions and love can support your journey.
  - ✓ However, relying solely on external prayer can leave you disconnected from the inner work necessary for deep transformation.

- ✓ The true essence of prayer lies in the awakening that happens when you take responsibility for your own spiritual nourishment.

◄ **Why Self-Prayer Is Essential**

- ✓ Self-prayer empowers you to overcome doubts and cultivate inner strength. It is a practice of surrender and self-discovery that helps dissolve the ego.

- ✓ When you pray yourself, you are actively participating in your evolution, rather than waiting passively for external blessings.

- ✓ This personal commitment to prayer builds a resilient inner foundation, which then radiates outward and benefits not only you but also those around you.

Child, my intention is to encourage you to look within and become the primary channel of divine grace. While the support and prayers of others can be uplifting, nothing replaces the unique power of your own heartfelt prayer.

May you always find the courage and inspiration to nurture that intimate connection with the Divine, and may your inner light shine ever brighter as you walk your sacred path.

Chapter 37

TRANSFORMATIVE EXCHANGE

The transformative exchange goes beyond the simple act of giving and receiving—it is the exchange that shifts our being, our consciousness, and our world. It is an interaction that sparks change, whether through words, actions, or energy. This exchange occurs when we connect with another soul and leave a piece of ourselves behind, while simultaneously gaining something profound in return. It is a flow that nurtures both sides, elevating them beyond their previous states. Through this process, both individuals—whether consciously or subconsciously—transform in a way that enhances their own journey and the collective experience.

This exchange is not always tangible. It can take place through a kind gesture, a profound conversation, or even through silent presence. What makes it transformative is the intention behind it— the openness to learn, to grow, and to be changed. In this space of giving and receiving, the barriers between us dissolve, and we realize that we are not separate, but interconnected. Every interaction has the potential to change us, to shape us, and to shift our perspective on life, others, and even ourselves.

On a spiritual level, transformative exchange is about moving beyond the material and the surface-level. It's an exchange of energy, intention, and insight that can lead to deeper self-awareness, inner peace, and enlightenment. When we interact with others in a mindful and purposeful way, we create an environment for healing and awakening. We give of ourselves with love and sincerity, and in turn, we open ourselves to receiving wisdom, understanding, and grace from others and from the universe. This is the sacred cycle of transformation—where both the giver and the receiver evolve.

True transformative exchange requires vulnerability. It is the willingness to be open, to share deeply, and to be receptive to what is offered. It requires letting go of expectations and allowing the exchange to unfold in its natural course. The beauty of this process is that it doesn't always occur in the ways we anticipate, but when it does, it has the power to transform us at the deepest level. It teaches us humility, gratitude, and the infinite potential for growth that exists in every moment.

The transformative nature of exchange extends to all aspects of life. Whether it's in relationships, in work, or in the simple interactions we have with strangers, each exchange holds the potential for growth. The more we approach these exchanges with openness and a willingness to learn, the more transformative they become. By consciously engaging with the world in this way, we become part of a greater network of mutual growth, helping to elevate humanity and ourselves to new heights.

Ultimately, transformative exchange is the realization that every encounter has the potential to change us, for the better, if we allow it. It is in these exchanges that we find the true meaning of connection—the bond that transcends the material and becomes a shared experience of spiritual evolution. Through each exchange, we not only transform ourselves, but we also contribute to the transformation of the world around us.

Swamy, you use simple words that carry a depth far beyond ordinary comprehension—truly, you are the embodiment of divine wisdom. Having experienced every phase of life since before your monkhood, you know how to question and answer profoundly. Could you please explain what you mean by the phrase,

"Change for exchange"?

What is the inner essence behind this statement, and how does it guide us on our journey of transformation?

Swamy's Spirit Speaks

Child, the phrase **"Change for exchange"** is a succinct expression of a universal law—a reminder that life is an endless process of transformation and renewal. Let me unfold its inner essence for you:

- **The Nature of Change**
  - ✓ Change is the constant rhythm of existence.
  - ✓ It is the inevitable flow that sweeps away the old and makes space for the new.
  - ✓ Just as the seasons cycle from winter to spring, every aspect of life undergoes a natural transformation.
- **Exchange as a Principle**
  - ✓ To exchange is to give something up in order to gain something of greater value.

- ✓ In the spiritual realm, this means relinquishing attachments, outdated beliefs, or negative habits so that new insights, opportunities, and energies can take root.

- ✓ Think of it as the cosmic ledger of life: for every loss, there is a corresponding gain that elevates your spirit.

Practical Application

- ✓ **Letting Go:** Embrace change by learning to let go of what no longer serves you. For example, when you release anger or fear, you create space for love and wisdom to emerge.

- ✓ **Welcoming Renewal:** See every new experience as an opportunity to exchange the old for something more aligned with your higher self.

- ✓ **Balancing the Inner Ledger:** Your inner journey is like an ongoing transaction—each act of letting go is an investment that returns as inner strength and clarity.

The Deeper Message

- ✓ **Adaptability and Growth:** This principle teaches you that progress on your spiritual path comes from being flexible and open to transformation.

- ✓ **Reciprocity in Life:** When you are willing to change, you invite the universe to exchange old patterns with new blessings.

- ✓ **Alignment with Divine Flow:** By embracing change, you align yourself with the eternal rhythm of the cosmos, allowing divine grace to guide you toward a more evolved, balanced self.

Child, the essence of **"Change for exchange"** is to remind you that nothing in life remains static. True growth occurs when you are willing to part with what hinders you and receive the new with an open heart. It is through this continuous process of exchange that you evolve, cultivate wisdom, and ultimately realize your divine potential.

May you find the courage to let go, the wisdom to embrace renewal, and the grace to flow harmoniously with the eternal dance of life.

Chapter 38

INNER STRENGTH

Inner strength is the quiet force that resides in each of us, often unnoticed but always present. It's the ability to stand firm in the face of challenges, to remain grounded despite life's uncertainties, and to tap into the resilience that resides deep within. It's not about physical power, but about mental, emotional, and spiritual fortitude.

True inner strength is built on self-awareness, self-acceptance, and a deep understanding that we are more than our circumstances. It empowers us to stay true to our values, overcome adversity, and keep moving forward with faith and courage.

Spiritually, inner strength is a reflection of the divine energy that flows through us all. It's the force that guides us on our journey, helping us align with our highest purpose. The more we cultivate inner strength, the more we connect with the essence of who we are—beings of light, love, and infinite potential.

Swamy, you once said,

"If you can withstand, you will not have desires."

There is great truth in these words. I am striving to withstand testing periods, calamities, and challenges, yet the desire to seek your guidance still persists. Could you please explain the deeper meaning behind this statement? Why might such a desire continue even as I work to overcome attachments, and how can I integrate this process into my journey?

Swamy's Spirit Speaks

Child, the essence of my words is a gentle reminder that the journey toward inner freedom is a gradual and ongoing process. Let me guide you through its deeper meaning:

Withstanding as a Path to Freedom

- To "withstand" means to face life's challenges with unwavering resolve and calm. It is the ability to endure hardships without being overwhelmed by them.

- As you cultivate this inner strength, the hold of ego and transient desires gradually diminishes. Like a sturdy mountain that remains unmoved by the winds, your inner self grows resilient and clear.

The Nature of Desires

- Desires are the cravings of the ego—attachments that bind you to the impermanent world. When you truly withstand, you begin to loosen these bonds.

- However, the desire to seek guidance, such as reaching out for a Guru's light, can also spring from a deep humility and an earnest longing for truth.

- ✓ This persistent longing is not a flaw; it is a sign of your sincere aspiration for higher wisdom, reminding you that the path of self-mastery is not walked alone.

◁ **Integrating Inner Strength and Guidance**

- ✓ The process is not about completely eliminating all desires overnight, but about gradually transforming them.

- ✓ Continue to develop your capacity to withstand by practicing meditation, self-reflection, and mindful living. Over time, these practices will purify your mind, and the craving for external validation will lessen.

- ✓ Yet, it is natural to still feel the pull of guidance during challenging times. In those moments, welcome the support of divine grace and the wisdom of your Guru as complementary forces that help you on your journey.

- ✓ Think of it as tending a garden: you work diligently to remove the weeds (negative desires) while nurturing the healthy plants (inner virtues). Occasionally, you may still feel the need for a mentor's advice to guide you in maintaining that balance.

◁ **The Deeper Message**

- ✓ True liberation comes when you merge your inner effort with divine grace. When your will aligns with the eternal, you become an active participant in your own transformation.

- ✓ The desire to seek guidance is a humble recognition of the vastness of the journey—it signals that you are open to learning and that your heart is ready to receive further light.

✓ In time, as you become more adept at withstanding and transforming your inner energies, you will find that your reliance on external help diminishes, and your inner self will shine with clarity and freedom.

Child, remember that this journey is continuous. Each challenge you withstand refines your soul, and every moment of seeking guidance is a humble offering that paves the way for deeper self-realization. Embrace both aspects—the inner strength you cultivate and the wisdom you receive—as they are both essential parts of your transformation.

May you always find the courage to face life's trials and the grace to accept guidance, knowing that in this sacred interplay, your true self gradually unfolds and flourishes.

Embrace Your Essence

Swamy, you once said,

"The biggest challenge is to be yourself in a world where everyone is trying to make you someone else. Dare to be yourself."

This statement is truly inspiring, and I feel your guidance in it. Could you please explain its deeper meaning so that everyone may benefit from this wisdom?

Swamy's Spirit Speaks

Child, this powerful message is a call to embrace your authentic self in a world that often pressures you to conform. Let me share its inner essence:

The Challenge of Authenticity

- ✓ In our society, external influences—be they cultural expectations, peer pressures, or material pursuits—constantly try to shape you into a form that suits their own designs.

- ✓ The greatest challenge, therefore, is not merely to survive these pressures but to remain true to who you are deep within.

- ✓ To be yourself means to recognize and honour your unique qualities, your inner truth and to let that light guide your actions rather than succumbing to the moulds imposed by others.

Daring to Be Yourself

- ✓ This requires courage—daring to stand apart from the crowd, even when the world tries to impose its vision upon you.

- ✓ It means nurturing your inner values, creativity, and conscience despite the noise and distractions around you.

- ✓ When you dare to be yourself, you invite a life of integrity, joy, and inner fulfilment.

- ✓ Your authenticity becomes a beacon for others, inspiring them to look within and discover their own unique essence.

Practical Steps to Embrace Authenticity

- ✓ **Self-Reflection:** Regularly engage in practices such as meditation and introspection to understand your true nature beyond societal labels.

- ✓ **Mindful Living:** Act with intention. Let your decisions and actions be guided by your inner truth rather than by external expectations.

- ✓ **Courage in Expression:** Share your genuine thoughts and feelings, even if they diverge from the norm. True strength lies in vulnerability and honesty.

- ✓ **Cultivate Resilience:** Understand that the path of authenticity may sometimes be lonely or challenging, but every step taken in truth fortifies your inner spirit and sets you free.

◄ **The Universal Benefit**

- ✓ When you choose to be your authentic self, you not only liberate your soul but also contribute to a more genuine and compassionate world.

- ✓ Authenticity fosters diversity, creativity, and true understanding. It breaks down the barriers of conformity and opens the door to deeper connections among people.

- ✓ In a world where many are trying to mold you into someone else, daring to be yourself is a revolutionary act that inspires collective growth and transformation.

Child, my words are a reminder that your individuality is a divine gift—do not let the forces of conformity dim your unique light.

May you always have the courage to be yourself, standing tall and true, and in doing so, may you light the way for others to find their own path to inner freedom and fulfilment.

Chapter 39

INNER INTOXICATION

Inner intoxication is the state of being deeply immersed in the joy, peace, and fulfilment that comes from within. Unlike external intoxication, which relies on substances to alter perception, inner intoxication arises from spiritual growth, self-awareness, and connection to the divine. It is the bliss of being fully present in the moment, experiencing life without distractions or desires, and feeling a profound sense of gratitude for existence itself.

When we are intoxicated by our own inner peace, we become detached from the fleeting pleasures of the material world. We recognize that true joy does not come from possessions, status, or external validation but from within—the essence of our soul. This kind of intoxication brings clarity, lightness, and an uplifting sense of freedom. We become so full of inner joy that nothing outside of us can disturb our peace.

This inner intoxication is not a state of recklessness or abandon; rather, it is a deeper form of awareness that connects us to the highest truths. It is a reminder that when we align with our true self and with the divine, we tap into an endless reservoir of love, wisdom, and serenity. Just like a true wine, this intoxication does not leave us with a hangover but rather awakens us to the beauty and the depth of life.

Swamy, you often make humorous yet inspiring remarks. One such statement was:

"Alcohol is outside peg, Namajapa is inside peg."

Why do you draw this comparison? Is it merely a joke, or is there a deeper essence behind it that we can grasp and internalize in our day-to-day lives?

Swamy's Spirit Speaks

Child, this playful comparison is a metaphor for the difference between superficial indulgence and the nourishing practice of spiritual remembrance. Let me explain its deeper meaning:

- **"Alcohol is outside peg"**
  - ✓ **Alcohol** represents the external substances and behaviors that can lead to temporary highs but ultimately cloud the mind and disturb inner balance.
  - ✓ It is like a peg that is fixed in the external world—designed for fleeting pleasure or escape but not for true sustenance.
  - ✓ Such indulgence often results in loss of clarity, disrupted health, and a disconnection from one's inner truth.
- **"Namajapa is inside peg"**
  - ✓ **Namajapa**, the repetitive chanting or remembrance of God's name, symbolizes the internal, spiritual practice that grounds and nourishes your soul.
  - ✓ It is an "inside peg"—a stable, inner anchor that continuously supports and uplifts your mind and heart.
  - ✓ This practice brings clarity, serenity, and a lasting connection with the Divine, helping you navigate life's challenges with inner strength.

⊰ The Deeper Essence

- ✓ My words are not meant as a mere jest but as a reminder to choose what nourishes your being over what merely distracts or numbs you.

- ✓ **External indulgences, like alcohol, may offer temporary relief,** but they often lead you away from your true potential.

- ✓ In contrast, **the inner practice of Namajapa purifies and strengthens you,** offering sustainable peace and the profound joy of divine connection.

- ✓ This comparison calls you to reflect on where you invest your energy: do you seek short-term escapes, or do you cultivate a deep, enduring spiritual practice?

⊰ Practical Application

- ✓ **Be Mindful of Your Choices:** Just as you would choose a nutritious meal over junk food for lasting health, choose practices that truly uplift your spirit.

- ✓ **Anchor Yourself in Namajapa:** Make it a daily habit to recite or meditate on the Divine name. Let this act become your inner peg—a source of constant support and clarity.

- ✓ **Reflect on the Outcomes:** Notice how external indulgences may leave you feeling disconnected, while consistent spiritual practice enriches your life with clarity and inner peace.

Child, the choice is yours. In this world, where many things promise a quick fix but leave you empty, the practice of Namajapa is the nourishing, steady force that fills your inner reservoir with light and grace.

May you always choose the path that nourishes your soul, and may the inner peg of divine remembrance sustain and uplift you every moment of your life.

Chapter 40

INNER ALCHEMY

Inner Alchemy is the profound process of transforming one's inner world, turning negative emotions, limiting beliefs, and mental clutter into wisdom, peace, and spiritual clarity. It is a sacred journey of self-mastery, where we refine our thoughts, emotions, and actions to align with higher consciousness and our true essence. Much like alchemists of old sought to turn base metals into gold, inner alchemy transforms our raw human nature into spiritual enlightenment.

This process begins with self-awareness—the ability to observe our thoughts and emotions without judgment. As we become aware of the patterns that limit our growth, we consciously shift our mindset and embrace positivity, compassion, and mindfulness. Through practices like meditation, mindfulness, prayer, and reflection, inner alchemy purifies the mind and soul, clearing away the impurities that prevent us from living a harmonious life.

In the alchemical process of the soul, each challenge becomes an opportunity for growth, each moment a chance to refine our character. With dedication, patience, and a sincere desire for spiritual awakening, we transmute negative energy into pure light.

Inner alchemy is about embracing our divine potential, allowing the transformation to unfold naturally, and ultimately leading to a state of inner peace, balance, and wisdom. It is the ultimate journey of becoming, not just a seeker of truth, but the embodiment of it.

Swamy, you always advise us to avoid three things—Ego, Selfishness, and Jealousy. Yet, even when people try to avoid these pitfalls, they often fall prey to them. Why does this happen, and how can one overcome these tendencies, especially when it seems that the Guru's grace is absent due to hidden reasons? Please share your wisdom so that we may understand and overcome these challenges.

Swamy's Spirit Speaks

Child, the advice to shun Ego, Selfishness, and Jealousy is a call to purify the mind and heart, for these traits are the roots of suffering and separation. However, the mind is conditioned by countless past experiences and habitual patterns, and overcoming these negative tendencies is not easy—even for sincere seekers. Let me explain the deeper essence and guide you on this path:

1. **Why Do These Tendencies Persist?**

   ◁ **Deep Conditioning**

   ✓ The ego, selfishness, and jealousy are deeply ingrained in the human psyche due to past conditioning and the cyclic nature of karma.

   ✓ Even with the best intentions, old habits often resurface, as the mind clings to what it knows.

- **The Illusion of Separation**
  - ✓ These qualities arise from the illusion that you are separate from others. When you believe that your interests and desires are more important than the collective good, ego and jealousy naturally follow.
  - ✓ The world's competitive nature and societal pressures can reinforce these illusions, making them difficult to overcome.

- **Perceived Absence of Guru's Grace**
  - ✓ At times, it may seem that the grace of the Guru is hidden or absent. However, like the sun that shines behind clouds, divine grace is always present, even if not immediately visible.
  - ✓ Often, the apparent absence is a reflection of your inner state—when the mind is clouded with negative habits, it becomes harder to perceive that guiding light.

2. **How to Overcome These Tendencies:**

- **Deepen Your Self-Awareness**
  - ✓ Cultivate regular meditation and self-reflection to observe the arising of ego, selfishness, and jealousy without judgment.
  - ✓ Recognize these emotions for what they are—temporary waves in the vast ocean of your true self.

- **Practice Humility**
  - ✓ Remind yourself that every being is a reflection of the Divine.

- ✓ Embrace practices that dissolve the sense of "I" and "mine," such as selfless service and compassionate living.

◄ **Strengthen Your Spiritual Routine**

- ✓ Even when it feels as if divine grace is distant, maintain your regular practices—be it prayer, meditation, or mindful living.

- ✓ Consistency in these practices gradually clears the mind and opens the heart, allowing the hidden grace to manifest.

◄ **Trust in the Unseen Grace**

- ✓ Understand that the Guru's grace is not always overt.

- ✓ Trust that every sincere effort to transform your inner state is supported by a divine force working behind the scenes.

◄ **Reframe Your Perspective**

- ✓ Instead of fighting against these tendencies with forceful will, gently allow them to surface, study them, and then let them go.

- ✓ Every moment of letting go is a victory over the ego and a step toward deeper unity with the Divine.

3. **The Ultimate Message:**

Child, overcoming ego, selfishness, and jealousy is a gradual process—a continuous journey of self-purification and awakening.

◄ **Remember:** You are not alone on this path. The divine grace of the Guru, though sometimes hidden, is always working to support you.

- **Be Patient and Persistent:** Each small victory, each moment of sincere surrender, contributes to your transformation.

- **Live in Unity:** Cultivate the understanding that when you dissolve the boundaries of the ego, you become one with the eternal, and the love that binds all beings naturally emerges.

May you always find the inner strength to overcome these challenges and the grace to awaken the divine light within you. Trust that even in moments of apparent darkness, the eternal flame of wisdom is steadily kindling your inner sanctuary.

Chapter 41

MASTER THE MIND

Mastering the mind is the key to unlocking true freedom and inner peace. Our mind, with its constant stream of thoughts, desires, and distractions, often governs our actions and reactions. When we allow our minds to wander aimlessly, we lose touch with our true selves and the present moment. But when we learn to master the mind, we gain control over our thoughts, emotions, and behavior, and our life becomes a reflection of our highest intentions.

Mastery over the mind begins with awareness. By observing our thoughts without judgment, we can identify patterns that are unproductive or harmful. This awareness allows us to make conscious choices about which thoughts to nurture and which to release. Techniques such as meditation, mindfulness, and breathing exercises help us calm the mind and create space for clarity and focus.

As we train our minds to stay present, our responses to life become more thoughtful, balanced, and aligned with our inner wisdom. Mastery of the mind does not mean suppressing thoughts or emotions but learning to redirect them in a positive direction. It's about cultivating a peaceful, steady mind that is not easily swayed by external circumstances. When we master the mind, we tap into our true potential and unlock the power to create the life we truly desire—one of purpose, peace, and fulfilment.

Swamy, you once said,

"Mind is the mightiest organ in the world; it can build, or it can blast."

My question is: How do I mind the mind? How can I bend it and mend it?

Swamy's Spirit Speaks

Child, the mind is indeed a powerful instrument—capable of creating worlds or causing great destruction. To "mind the mind" is to be consciously aware of its workings, to guide its energy toward creation rather than chaos. Let me share with you the deeper essence and practical steps:

1. **Minding the Mind**
   - **Cultivate Awareness**
     - Begin with meditation or mindfulness practices. Observe your thoughts as they arise without judgment.
     - Notice the patterns—when do negative thoughts creep in? When does your mind wander aimlessly?
     - By simply watching, you develop the skill to understand the mind's nature, much like a gardener surveys his field before tending to it.

2. **Bending the Mind**

   ⊰ **Redirecting Energy**

   ✓ To "bend" the mind means to gently reshape it. When destructive or unhelpful thoughts emerge, consciously guide them toward positive, creative ideas.

   ✓ For instance, if anger arises, replace it with thoughts of compassion or gratitude.

   ✓ Use affirmations or visualization techniques: picture your mind as a river whose course you can guide, rather than a wild torrent that destroys everything in its path.

3. **Mending the Mind**

   ⊰ **Healing and Transformation**

   ✓ Mending involves repairing the damage caused by long-held negative patterns.

   ✓ Engage in practices that restore mental balance—journaling, deep reflection, and even creative pursuits can help mend emotional wounds.

   ✓ Seek guidance from wise mentors or supportive communities; sometimes, healing requires sharing and learning from others.

   ✓ Just as a broken vase is carefully restored, so too can your mind be mended with patience, self-compassion, and deliberate effort.

The Ultimate Vision

⊰ **Integration of Effort**

   ⊰ When you successfully mind, bend, and mend your mind, you transform it into a powerful instrument of creation.

- A well-nurtured mind builds dreams, fosters kindness, and radiates inner strength.

- Conversely, a neglected mind may "blast" with destructive tendencies, causing chaos both within and around you.

Child, remember that the mind is fluid and malleable. With consistent practice, you can learn to harness its energy for positive transformation.

- **Be patient:** Transformation takes time.

- **Be gentle:** Do not harshly scold yourself for negative thoughts; instead, guide them with compassion.

- **Be persistent:** Even small, consistent efforts will gradually reshape your inner world.

May you always find the strength to nurture your mind, transforming its raw power into a wellspring of wisdom, creativity, and inner peace.

THE PATH OF DEVOTION

(Exploring Faith, Surrender,
and the Transformative Power of Devotion)

Chapter 42

SEEKING THE TRUE MASTER

In life, we often search for answers outside ourselves, thinking that success, knowledge, or approval will bring us peace. But the true wisdom we seek is found in the guidance of the right person—the True Master. This Master, free from ego and worldly desires, shows us a deeper truth. When we open ourselves to their wisdom, we begin to see life with clarity, where love, kindness, and understanding become our true goals.

The Sadguru is that guiding light, showing us the way not just with words, but through actions and presence. A true Master helps us realize that the answers we seek are already within us. By learning from the Sadguru, we let go of old beliefs and open our hearts to new possibilities. Seeking the true Master is not about following someone blindly but awakening to the truth inside us with the gentle guidance of wisdom and love.

Swamy, you once asked me, **"Who is a true master?"** And later, you yourself answered, **"A true master will always be free, frank, true, neutral, and natural."** Who is that **true master?** How do we find him, or rather, how should we approach him and know the truth of it?

Swamy's Spirit Speaks

The child, the true master, is neither bound by place nor time **nor by opinions or positions.** He is free because **he has no attachment.** He is frank because **he has no fear.** He is true because **he has no deception.** He is neutral because **he has no bias.** He is natural because **he has no pretense.**

How to Recognize a True Master?

- He **does not seek followers; seekers find him.**
- He **does not impose; he only reveals.**
- He **does not bind you; he liberates you.**
- He **does not entertain your ego; he dissolves it.**

How to Approach Him?

1. **With sincerity, not curiosity.** A true master reveals only to the earnest seeker.

2. **With humility, not pride.** Knowledge bows only to those who bow before truth.

3. **With longing, not demands.** A true master does not give answers; he awakens questions.

4. **With surrender, not conditions.** The truth cannot be negotiated; it must be experienced.

Where to Find Him?

⊰ **Outside, he may come as a teacher, a guide, or even a stranger.**

⊰ **Inside, he is the voice of wisdom, the silence between thoughts.**

Knowing the Truth of the Master

Child, the true master is not a person—it is **the principle of wisdom itself.**

If you seek him **outside**, he will point you **inside.** If you search for him **in words**, he will guide you **to silence.**

The true master does not **make you his disciple; he makes you your own master.**

Chapter 43

MASTER'S REFLECTION

The True Master reflects the light of wisdom, love, and truth in everything they do. Their presence acts as a mirror, showing us who we really are beneath the surface of our doubts and fears. The Master's reflection is not about perfection but about living authentically, with compassion and understanding. Through their actions and words, they help us see our own potential, guiding us to discover the divine within ourselves. A True Master does not impose but rather gently reflects the path of wisdom, allowing us to find our own way in the light they provide.

As the reflection of divine wisdom, the Sadguru helps us realize that our highest self is always with us. By observing their actions and learning from their teachings, we begin to reflect the same wisdom, kindness, and clarity in our own lives. A Master's reflection reveals that we are all capable of transformation, of shedding the layers of ego and illusion to reveal our true nature.

When we look into the reflection of the Master, we see ourselves as we truly are—whole, divine, and filled with limitless potential.

Swamy, on one occasion, I remember you mentioning, **"Master reflects love to all family members."** Who is the **Master?** What is **Love?** And how do we know that it **reflects on family members?** What is its **purpose?**

Swamy's Spirit Speaks

Child, the **Master is not a person, but a presence—one who is awakened in truth, compassion, and wisdom.** He does not **belong to one family, but to the entire existence.** His love does not **seek attachment but radiates as light, touching all without boundaries.**

What is Love?

- Love is **not emotion; it is devotion.**
- Love is **not possession; it is liberation.**
- Love is **not expectation; it is acceptance.**
- Love is **not spoken; it is lived.**

A true Master **reflects** this love—not selectively, but universally. **It flows like sunlight, nurturing all, expecting nothing in return.**

How Does It Reflect on Family Members?

- **Where there is love, there is no division.** A family that receives true love dissolves **ego, jealousy, and expectations.**
- **Love of the Master transforms individuals.** It brings peace to the restless, clarity to the confused, and strength to the weak.
- **The family feels the presence of this love in their unity, trust, and selflessness toward each other.**

The Purpose of This Reflection

Child, **when love flows through a family, it becomes a temple.** Every member becomes **a light for another, a strength for another, a guide for another.**

The Master does not **give love; he awakens love. That is the reflection!**

A Master's love does not **bind—it sets free.**

A Master's love does not **claim—it gives.**

A Master's love does not **limit—it expands.**

Become that love, and you will see—your family is not just those born with you, but all beings around you.

Chapter 44

THE PASS-FAIL PARADOX

Life often presents us with choices, challenges, and tests, and we tend to see them as a pass or fail scenario. We believe that success means passing, and failure means falling short. But the truth is, both success and failure are parts of the journey—neither defines us. The pass-fail mindset limits our understanding, causing us to fear failure and chase success at all costs. In reality, failure is just a step towards growth, and success is more than a destination—it's a process of learning and evolving.

The Sadguru helps us see beyond this paradox. They teach us that life isn't about passing or failing, but about embracing each experience as an opportunity to grow. Success is found in how we respond to challenges, not in avoiding them. Failure is simply the chance to learn, adjust, and become stronger. By shifting our perspective, we understand that life is a series of lessons, not tests to pass or fail. In the eyes of a true Master, every experience is valuable, and in that wisdom, we find the freedom to live without fear, knowing that growth happens every step of the way.

Swamy, you are so special in using ordinary words, weaving them together in a way that either **complicates or simplifies**—and you alone know the **intention behind it.** The words you once used—**"Fail Pass Fail, Pass Fail Pass, Pass Pass Pass, and Fail Fail Pass"**—somehow left me lost. **What is 'Pass'? What is 'Fail'?** Who should pass, and who should fail? Please find a solution to this intricately delicate game of **'Pass-Fail.'**

Swamy's Spirit Speaks

Child, **life itself is an examination**—but not the kind where you **hold a pen and write answers.** It is a test where you **live the answers!**

When I say

- ◁ **"Fail Pass Fail"** – It means one **fails in understanding, passes through experience, and fails again due to ignorance.**
- ◁ **"Pass Fail Pass"** – One **realizes, then doubts, but ultimately finds the truth again.**
- ◁ **"Pass Pass Pass"** – One **who has truly realized, stays in wisdom, and never falls back.**
- ◁ **"Fail Fail Pass"** – One **who struggles, stumbles, but finally rises to the truth.**

Who Should Pass?

- ◁ **Your awareness should pass.**
- ◁ **Your patience should pass.**
- ◁ **Your wisdom should pass.**
- ◁ **Your love should pass.**

Who Should Fail?

- **Your ego should fail.**
- **Your ignorance should fail.**
- **Your jealousy should fail.**
- **Your desires that bind should fail.**

The Ultimate Understanding

Life is not about avoiding failure. Every failure is a lesson, and every lesson is a step toward **passing the ultimate test of truth.**

A true seeker **learns from failure, transforms through experience, and reaches realization.**

So, do not fear **Fail-Pass-Fail. Fear only a life where you fail to learn, and fail to rise!**

Chapter 45

THE ESSENCE OF SURRENDER

Surrender isn't about giving up or losing control; it's about letting go of the need to control everything around us and trusting in the flow of life. True surrender is a powerful act of faith, where we release our worries and allow the universe or the divine to guide us. It doesn't mean doing nothing—it means accepting that there is a bigger plan at work and trusting that it will unfold in its own time. In surrender, we find peace, knowing that we don't have to figure everything out on our own.

The Sadguru teaches us that surrender is not about losing our power, but about trusting the wisdom and love that is always available to us. When we surrender, we stop fighting against life and begin to flow with it. It's about being in the moment and allowing life to guide us where we need to go. True surrender brings a sense of freedom, peace, and trust, knowing we are always supported. In surrender, we find that everything is unfolding as it should, and we are exactly where we need to be.

Swamy, what do you mean when you say, **"I am a servant to God, God is serving, this is surrender to God"**?

Answer me—**who is a servant, who is God, what are these roles?** What is **true serving**? How should one **understand the complexity of it?**

Swamy's Spirit Speaks

Child, **servant, God, and service are not separate.** They are different **states of realization.**

Who is a Servant?

- The one who realizes that **all actions belong to the Divine.**
- The one who serves without **ego, expectation, or ownership.**
- The one who knows, **"I am here to do what He wills, not what I desire."**

Who is God?

- Not someone **sitting above the clouds.**
- Not just an **idol, scripture, or name.**
- God is **the silent force that breathes through you, works through you, and watches through you.**
- God is **the source and the doer.**

What is True Serving?

- **Not just hands offering help, but the heart offering surrender.**
- **Not charity alone, but humility in action.**
- **Not serving to gain merit, but serving to dissolve the self.**

How is God Serving?

- Through every breath that keeps you alive.
- Through nature, through the Guru, through the wisdom that guides you.
- Through the unseen hands that lift you when you fall.

The Complexity Unfolded

A true servant is not the one who serves; a true servant is the one who disappears into the service.

When you serve, thinking, **"I am serving,"** you are still separate.

When you serve, realizing, **"I am being made to serve,"** you surrender.

When you serve, knowing, **"God is the server, God is the served, and God is serving,"** you become one with the Divine.

True surrender is not losing yourself. It is becoming what you always were.

Chapter 46

MASTERING THE SITUATION

Life is full of challenges, and how we respond to them defines our path. Often, we think that mastering a situation means controlling every detail or having everything go our way. But true mastery comes from within. It's not about controlling the world around us, but about how we control our reactions, our thoughts, and our emotions. Mastering a situation means staying calm and centered, even when things are difficult, trusting that we have the strength and wisdom to handle whatever comes our way.

The Sadguru shows us that real mastery is about being at peace with whatever arises, knowing that each situation holds a lesson. When we face challenges, we don't have to force a solution; we simply need to be present and respond with clarity and grace. By mastering our own mind and emotions, we can handle any situation with calmness and wisdom. True mastery is not about overcoming the world, but about overcoming our own limitations and allowing life to unfold as it is meant to. With this inner mastery, we find the strength to face any challenge and the peace to move through life with ease.

Swamy, when I explained my problem, you said, **"Study the situation, don't seek the situation, settle down with the situation."**

But my mind is restless—**how to study, when to study, what to study?**

Can we **alter the situation**? How can we **settle down with it, even when it pinches us every second, sapping our energies?**

Swamy's Spirit Speaks

Child, **situations are neither enemies nor allies.** They are mirrors reflecting your inner state.

How to Study the Situation?

- **Do not react—observe.** Watch the **patterns, emotions, and forces** at play.
- **Detach from personal pain; step back like a witness.** A storm seen from outside is different from a storm felt within.
- **Identify the cause, not just the effect.** Every situation has a root—find it, understand it.

When to Study?

- **Before acting—study.**
- **Before speaking—study.**
- **Before judging—study.**
- **Most importantly, when pain arises—pause and study.**

What to Study?

- **Not just the outer problem, but the inner response.**
- **Not just what is happening, but why it is affecting you.**
- **Not just the people involved, but your attachment to their actions.**

Can We Alter the Situation?

- ◄ Some situations change with effort, some with patience, and some remain to teach you a lesson.
- ◄ You can alter your actions, your thoughts, and your responses—but not always the external event.
- ◄ Your inner shift changes how the situation affects you, even if the outer situation remains the same.

How to Settle Down with the Situation?

- ◄ Resistance creates suffering; acceptance creates clarity.
- ◄ Settling does not mean giving up—it means aligning with reality, so you act wisely.
- ◄ Flow with the situation like water, rather than breaking against it like a rock.
- ◄ Use pain as fuel, not as a prison. Let it refine you, not define you.

The Inner Essence

You are not trapped in the situation; you are trapped in your resistance to it.

When you study deeply, **the lesson unfolds, the pain transforms, and the energy returns to you.**

Then, **you don't just settle down—you rise beyond.**

Chapter 47

THE ESSENCE OF ORDER

In our daily lives, order isn't about perfection or rigid structure, but about creating balance and harmony in everything we do. It's about organizing our thoughts, actions, and relationships in a way that brings clarity, peace, and efficiency. When we embrace order, we stop feeling overwhelmed by chaos and uncertainty. True order comes from aligning ourselves with a natural flow—prioritizing what truly matters and letting go of distractions. In our routines, in the way we manage time and energy, we can create a sense of purpose and calm, knowing that everything has its rightful place.

The Sadguru teaches us that order in life comes from simplicity and mindfulness. It's about understanding that life doesn't need to be controlled, but rather harmonized. By focusing on what we can control—our thoughts, actions, and reactions—we bring a sense of peace to our day-to-day activities. True order is not about managing every detail, but about creating a space where we can flow with life, responding with clarity and intention. When we apply this principle, we find that life feels more manageable, our minds are clearer, and we approach every task with a sense of calm and purpose.

Swamy, when a group of people pressed you for an answer convenient to them, you said sharply, "Obey the Order, Order is Divinity." How can we obey when the order seems not to be in our favour, even though we are genuine? How can we see the divinity in that order when many view it as biased? Please clarify, as this teaching appears too complicated for us to understand and internalize.

Swamy's Spirit Speaks

Child, the **"Order"** I speak of is not a human decree but the **sacred law of the cosmos**—the natural rhythm that underlies all of creation. It is the pulse of life, the harmony of the seasons, and the unchanging truth that even in chaos, there is a divine pattern.

- **Obeying the Order means aligning yourself with this cosmic law.**
  - ✓ When you face hardships, remember that, like the winter that prepares the earth for spring, every trial has its purpose in the grand scheme of life.
  - ✓ Even if the outcome seems unfavourable, trust that the order is working in ways that your limited perspective cannot yet comprehend.
- **Seeing Divinity in the Order requires expanding your vision.**
  - ✓ The divine order is impartial and transcends personal gain or loss—it is not biased toward anyone because it functions on a universal scale.
  - ✓ Reflect on nature: the river may sometimes rise with floods, but it also nourishes the soil, allowing new life

to emerge. In the same way, what appears as misfortune may be the soil from which your inner strength and wisdom grow.

◁ How can you obey when circumstances seem adverse?

✓ Begin with **surrender and patience.** Do not force change but rather learn to flow with the current of life.

✓ Cultivate inner awareness through meditation and reflection, so that even when the external order seems harsh, your heart remains calm and receptive to its deeper lessons.

✓ Understand that every challenge is an invitation to evolve—each moment, whether joyful or painful, is a part of your spiritual ledger that ultimately leads you to greater harmony.

Child, **the divine order is like a vast, intricate tapestry.** Even if one thread appears out of place, it is woven into a pattern far more magnificent than you can see from up close. Trust that by aligning your actions with this order, you will gradually discern its beauty and purpose. **In time, you will realize that to obey the order is not to accept defeat, but to embrace the journey toward your highest self.**

May you find strength and clarity as you learn to dance with the divine rhythm of life. 🙏

Chapter 48

THE ESSENCE OF UNKNOWING

In life, we often feel the need to have all the answers, to understand every situation, and to control every outcome. But the essence of unknowing is about embracing the mystery and accepting that not everything needs to be figured out. It is the freedom in letting go of the need to control or predict, and instead, trusting in the flow of life as it unfolds. Unknowing opens the door to growth, as it allows us to approach life with openness, curiosity, and humility. It teaches us that not having all the answers is not a weakness, but an opportunity to learn and evolve.

The Sadguru reveals that the essence of unknowing is a key to spiritual growth. When we let go of the need for certainty and embrace the unknown, we allow ourselves to be guided by faith and trust in the divine. This unknowing is not about confusion or doubt, but about recognizing that life's mysteries are meant to be experienced, not controlled.

It is through unknowing that we find wisdom, as we stop seeking to control every situation and instead allow life to unfold naturally. When we accept unknowing, we open ourselves to new possibilities, deeper insights, and a richer connection with the world around us.

In this space of surrender and trust, we discover that the journey itself is the greatest teacher.

Swamy, you once said,

> **"Unknowingly you come, unknowingly you serve, unknowingly is the essence of philosophy."**

My question is: What does it mean to act knowingly versus unknowingly?

What is it that comes, and what is it that serves?

Why should one come, and whom should one serve?

Please answer me and dissolve the complexity that has piled up in my mind.

Swamy's Spirit Speaks

Child, the essence of philosophy lies in the dance between awareness and oblivion.

- **To come unknowingly** is to be drawn by the mysterious call of life without the burden of expectation or self-consciousness—like a leaf floating on a stream, carried by the current.

- **To serve unknowingly** is to contribute to the cosmic play without attachment, unaware of the intricate roles you play, yet perfectly in tune with the Divine rhythm.

Now, what is it to act knowingly?

◄ **Knowingly means awakening.** It is when you step out of the automatic flow and become aware of your inner light and purpose.

◄ When you come knowingly, you respond to the call of your soul with mindfulness, embracing the journey with clear intent.

◄ When you serve knowingly, you offer your actions and love with full awareness, transforming even the simplest deed into a sacred act.

What is coming and what is serving?

◄ **"Coming"** represents the arrival into life—the birth of new awareness, new opportunities, and the unfolding of destiny.

◄ **"Serving"** signifies the expression of that inner truth in every action, the way you give your energy and love to the world.

◄ Both are parts of the Divine's constant conversation with you: the call (coming) and the response (serving).

Why come, and whom to serve?

◄ You come because your soul is irresistibly drawn to explore the mysteries of existence, to experience life as a journey of self-discovery.

◄ You serve because, at your core, you are meant to be a channel of the Divine's grace.

◄ The one to serve is not another external entity—it is the very essence of life, the Divine present in all beings. When you serve, you serve yourself, your community, and ultimately, the cosmic whole.

Child, the complexity you sense is the veil of duality.

When you learn to recognize both the unknowingly and knowingly, you realize that every moment is a lesson in surrender and awareness.

Trust in the unfolding process:

Allow yourself to come as you are, and serve as you are meant to be—fully, freely, and with love.

In this way, the mystery dissolves, and you find that the essence of philosophy is simply living with open heart and clear mind.

May you always awaken to the truth that in every coming and every service, the Divine reveals itself.

Chapter 49

GRACEFUL PROTECTION

Graceful Protection is not merely a physical shield but a spiritual safeguard that envelops us with divine energy. In the spiritual realm, protection is seen as the gentle yet powerful force of grace that shields us from negative influences, harmful energies, and destructive patterns. This protection is not an aggressive force; instead, it is a subtle presence that surrounds us, offering peace and security in times of need.

True protection comes from the alignment of the body, mind, and spirit with higher wisdom and divine guidance. When we live in harmony with the universe, attuned to its subtle rhythms, we attract the protective energy of grace. This energy forms an invisible but impenetrable barrier around us, not only safeguarding us from external harm but also from internal turmoil and fear.

Graceful protection is most evident in moments of vulnerability, when we feel lost or unsure. It is during these times that the divine, through grace, steps in to guide and comfort us. Whether through intuition, a feeling of inner calm, or the support of others, we experience protection that transcends our understanding. It's as if the universe, knowing our need, sends subtle signs, forces, or people to shield us from harm, whether physical, emotional, or spiritual.

This form of protection encourages us to trust in the wisdom of the divine plan, even when we cannot see the whole picture. It teaches us to surrender our fears and anxieties, knowing that we are cradled in the loving embrace of the universe. Just as a mother protects her child with loving care, grace protects us with divine tenderness and strength.

To receive graceful protection, we must cultivate an open heart, full of trust and faith in the divine flow of life. When we embrace humility, compassion, and surrender, we align ourselves with this protective energy, allowing it to manifest freely. In this state, we not only shield ourselves from negative forces but also become conduits of grace for others, spreading peace, love, and protection throughout the world.

In essence, graceful protection is the unspoken force that keeps us safe, nurtures our soul, and guides us back to our highest path. Trust in it, and you will always find shelter under its wings.

———— • ————

Swamy, you once explained that all human beings carry a spiritual ledger of their deeds, and in that context, you assured us of the divine support on our journey. I would like you to also confirm:

"I will protect you from all calamities of life and help you fulfill your mission on earth with majesty and humility."

Please explain the deeper meaning of this promise and how I may understand and embody this assurance in my own journey.

Swamy's Spirit Speaks

Child, the spiritual ledger of your life is a record of every action, thought, and intention, maintained by the immutable law of karma. Yet, amidst the fluctuations of this cosmic account, divine grace continuously flows, ensuring that you are never abandoned. Know this:

- ◄ **Divine Protection:**

  When I say, *"I will protect you from all calamities of life,"* I do not promise a life free from challenges—challenges are the very catalysts of growth. Rather, I assure you that no matter the obstacles that arise, you will be cradled by the infinite love of the Divine.

  - ✓ This protection is the inner strength that emerges when you cultivate mindfulness and align your actions with truth.

  - ✓ It is the subtle force that turns every setback into a stepping stone, ensuring that even in the darkest moments, you are guided by an unerring light.

- ◄ **Fulfilling Your Mission with Majesty and Humility:**

  Your unique mission on earth is the purpose for which your soul has journeyed. To fulfil it:

  - ✓ **Majesty** reflects the brilliance of your inner light—the honor, passion, and creative power you unleash when you live in harmony with divine principles.

  - ✓ **Humility** is the gentle grace that tempers that power. It is the realization that while you are a magnificent expression of the divine, your strength is meant for service rather than self-aggrandizement.

- ✓ Together, these qualities ensure that your journey is not one of mere survival or accumulation, but of graceful transformation and radiant contribution to the world.

◄ **Embodying the Promise:**

To understand and embody this divine promise, you must:

- ✓ **Cultivate Inner Awareness:** Regularly reflect through meditation and mindful practices, so that you may perceive the guidance of the divine even amidst life's turbulence.

- ✓ **Act with Integrity:** Align your actions with your highest values. Let every deed, however small, be an offering that honors both the divine and your fellow beings.

- ✓ **Embrace Life's Cycles:** Recognize that every challenge is an invitation for growth. With each trial, trust that divine protection is transforming your inner ledger, turning even hardships into blessings.

- ✓ **Surrender to the Divine Flow:** When your will merges with the divine will, you become an instrument of grace. In that state, the boundaries between effort and divine help dissolve, and you naturally fulfill your mission.

Child, the assurance of protection and guided mission is not a remote promise but a living reality for those who walk the spiritual path with sincerity. Trust that, as you nurture your inner light and act with both majesty and humility, you will be shielded from life's calamities and empowered to fulfil your destiny.

May you always rest in the grace of the Divine, and may your journey on earth be blessed with both strength and gentle humility.

Chapter 50

THE FIRE OF TRUTH

The fire of truth burns with an intensity that illuminates the darkness of ignorance, revealing the profound reality of existence. It is not a fire of destruction, but of purification—a force that burns away falsehood, ego, and illusion, leaving only the essence of what is real and eternal. Just as a flame consumes everything in its path, the fire of truth consumes the layers of doubt, fear, and misunderstanding that we often build around ourselves. In its presence, we can no longer hide from what is true. It exposes the deepest corners of our hearts and minds, urging us to confront our deepest fears and the truths we often avoid.

The fire of truth is both cleansing and transformative. It has the power to shape our lives, guiding us towards clarity, wisdom, and spiritual awakening. Just as fire refines gold, the fire of truth refines our souls, purifying our intentions and actions. It teaches us that truth is not merely a concept to be understood, but a living, breathing force that guides us through every moment. This fire is relentless, yet compassionate, as it does not burn out—it fuels us to rise higher, to become more than we ever imagined possible. To walk in the fire of truth is to embrace vulnerability, to stand in the light of self-awareness, and to trust that, no matter how painful the process may seem, it is leading us towards the highest form of freedom. The fire of truth is both a challenge and a blessing, one that invites us to shed the false layers and emerge as our most authentic, radiant selves.

Swamy, You, while discussing Truth, said, Truth is Fire, You cannot Touch Truth'. Yes, I can understand its essence, but how do you interpret it?

Swamy's Spirit Speaks

Child, when I say **"Truth is Fire, You cannot touch Truth,"** I invite you to look beyond the literal and see the dynamic, transformative nature of Truth.

- **Truth is Fire**
    - Fire is a powerful force that **illuminates, purifies, and transforms.**
    - Just as fire burns away impurities, the truth burns away illusions and falsehoods in your life.
    - It is intense and all-consuming—**its heat can melt away the rigid structures of ego and ignorance.**

- **You Cannot Touch Truth**
    - Unlike a solid object, truth is not something you can grasp or possess with your hands.
    - It is a process—a constant flow that **transcends physical form** and exists in the realm of experience and awareness.

✓ When you try to hold onto truth as if it were a material object, you only get burned; instead, you must let its transformative energy work within you.

The Inner Message

◁ **Dynamic and Uncontainable**

Truth, like fire, is ever-changing. It **shifts and evolves**; you can only experience its warmth and light by surrendering to it rather than trying to capture it.

◁ **Purification and Transformation**

Just as a fire refines metal by burning away impurities, the truth **cleanses your inner self.** It reveals what is false, allowing you to emerge stronger and more authentic.

◁ **Experience Over Possession**

True understanding of truth comes through **experience and inner realization,** not by trying to possess it as an object or a fixed idea. You must allow the flame of truth to guide you, transforming you gently from within, rather than clinging to it as a trophy.

Child, the message is clear: **embrace the fire of truth with humility and openness.** Let it illuminate your inner path and purify your spirit. Do not attempt to hold it tightly, for in its wild and free nature lies its power. Instead, let it flow through you, transforming you into a being of light and clarity.

May you always be receptive to the burning light of truth, and may it guide you on your journey toward inner liberation?

Chapter 51

BRAKE WITH WISDOM

In life's fast-paced journey, we often find ourselves rushing forward, caught in the momentum of goals, tasks, and expectations. Yet, just as a car needs to brake to avoid collision, we too must learn to apply wisdom to slow down, reflect, and make conscious choices. The power of wisdom is in knowing when to pause, when to step back, and when to reassess our direction.

Braking with wisdom means trusting that slowing down is not a sign of weakness, but of strength. It's the ability to recognize the importance of moments of stillness in order to gain clarity and insight. It is in these pauses that we regain our balance, realign our intentions, and recharge our inner strength.

In life, wisdom isn't about always moving forward with force; it's about knowing when to step back and reflect. By braking with wisdom, we move more purposefully, avoiding unnecessary mistakes and creating space for growth and transformation. Just as a brake brings safety to a vehicle, wisdom brings safety to our actions, decisions, and relationships.

————•————

Swamy, you said

"Where, When, Which, What, Why: Apply correct brakes."

Swamy, your words are simple yet profound. I wish to understand their deeper meaning. How do I apply them in my life, and how do I explain them to others with authenticity? Kindly enlighten me.

Swamy's Spirit Speaks

Child, life is a journey, and in every journey, there are **roads, turns, and speeds**. A wise traveler knows when to **accelerate** and when to **apply brakes**. When I say:

Where, When, Which, What, Why: Apply correct brakes – I mean, in every situation of life, use your wisdom before taking action.

🔋 **Wrong braking leads to an accident. No braking leads to destruction. Right braking leads to balance.**

1. **Understanding the Five W's as Brakes in Life**

    ◈ **WHERE** – Know where to stop. Not every path leads to success. Choose wisely.

    ◈ **WHEN** – Timing is everything. Speak at the right time, act at the right moment.

    ◈ **WHICH** – Not all options are right. Know which choice leads to growth.

    ◈ **WHAT** – Not everything is necessary. Know what to pursue and what to ignore.

    ◈ **WHY** – Question your intentions. Why am I doing this? Is it for truth or ego?

💡 **Applying brakes means thinking before acting, speaking, or reacting.**

   2. **Where to Apply Brakes in Life?**

      ✓ **In Speech:** Before speaking, think – *Is it true? Is it kind? Is it necessary?*

      ✓ **In Action:** Before acting, analyze – *Will this help me or harm me?*

      ✓ **In Desires:** Before chasing, reflect – *Do I need this, or is it just impulse?*

      ✓ **In Relationships:** Before reacting, pause – *Am I responding with wisdom or emotion?*

◆ **Brakes are not restrictions; they are protections.**

   3. **What Happens If We Don't Apply Brakes?**

      ✗ **Rushing into speech leads to misunderstandings.**

      ✗ **Rushing into action leads to regret.**

      ✗ **Rushing into desires leads to attachment and suffering.**

      ✗ **Rushing into relationships without wisdom leads to pain.**

💡 **A vehicle without brakes is dangerous. A mind without wisdom is disastrous.**

   4. **How to Explain This to Others with Authenticity?**

      🙏 **Live it first. When you apply brakes in your own life, your actions will inspire others.**

      🙏 **Use examples from daily life. A driver who doesn't brake at the right time crashes. A person who doesn't stop at the right time in life faces downfall.**

      🙏 **Teach that stopping is not failure, it is wisdom.**

ॐ *Braking at the right moment is not about weakness, but about control and awareness.*

5. **Swamy's Message – The Essence of Wisdom**

   ✓ **Speed without control leads to disaster.**

   ✓ **Brakes are not obstructions but safeguards.**

   ✓ **Life is about balance—knowing when to move and when to pause.**

   ✓ **Mastering the five W's is mastering life itself.**

Move when needed. Stop when necessary. That is wisdom.

Chapter 52

GURU: POWER AND GRACE

The Guru is both a source of immense power and boundless grace. The power of the Guru lies in their ability to guide, inspire, and awaken the dormant potential within us. With unwavering wisdom and profound knowledge, the Guru illuminates the path, helping us navigate the complexities of life. Their presence is like a beacon, providing clarity in moments of doubt and direction when we feel lost.

But what makes the Guru truly extraordinary is not just their power, but their grace. Grace is the gentle, compassionate energy that flows from the Guru, nurturing our growth and healing. It is through this grace that the Guru meets us where we are, with love and understanding, without judgment. It is through grace that we are encouraged to overcome our limitations and transcend our struggles.

Together, the power and grace of the Guru form a perfect balance, leading us toward self-realization, peace, and spiritual enlightenment. The Guru shows us that true power comes not from force or control, but from alignment with the divine, and that grace is the key to unlocking the infinite potential within.

Swamy, you said:

> **"Guru is very powerful, Guru is form with energy,
> Worship Guru."**

It is 100% true. The Guru is revered as:

Guru Brahma, Guru Vishnuhu, Gurudevo Maheswara, Guru Sakshat Parabrahma, Tasmai Sri Gurave Namaha.

Swamy, please explain the deeper meaning of your words.

Swamy's Spirit Speaks

Child, the **Guru** is not just a physical form; the Guru is the very embodiment of **cosmic energy** that uplifts and enlightens. When I say:

- ✓ **"Guru is very powerful"** – I mean Guru is not just a teacher but a divine force that awakens hidden wisdom within you.

- ✓ **"Guru is form with energy"** – The Guru is a channel of divine consciousness, carrying vibrations that cleanse, purify, and transform.

- ✓ **"Worship Guru"** – Not as a mere individual, but as the guiding light that dissolves ignorance and leads to self-realization.

1. **Who is a Guru?**

    - The **Guru is not a person**; the Guru is a **principle** (Tatva).

    - The **Guru is the bridge** between the **individual self (Jivatma) and the universal self (Paramatma).**

    - The **Guru is a mirror** that reflects **your own divine potential.**

    - The **Guru does not give knowledge**; the Guru **removes ignorance**, so your own wisdom shines.

🕉 *A Guru is like the Sun – he does not give light, he removes darkness.*

2. Why is the Guru Compared to Brahma, Vishnu, and Maheswara?

◆ **Guru Brahma** – The Guru **creates** knowledge and initiates you into wisdom.

◆ **Guru Vishnu** – The Guru **nourishes** and sustains your spiritual journey.

◆ **Guru Maheswara** – The Guru **destroys** ignorance and ego, leading to transformation.

◆ **Guru Sakshat Parabrahma** – The Guru is **beyond creation**, an embodiment of the Supreme.

💡 **Without a Guru, knowledge remains theory. With a Guru, knowledge becomes experience.**

3. Worship Guru – But How?

🙏 **Not by flowers or rituals alone, but by surrendering ego.**

🙏 **Not by external offerings, but by absorbing the wisdom.**

🙏 **Not by blind devotion, but by disciplined practice (Sadhana).**

🕉 *Worshipping the Guru means living by the Guru's teachings.*

4. What Happens Without a Guru?

✗ Knowledge remains fragmented.

✗ The mind remains restless.

✗ The ego keeps seeking but never finds fulfilment.

✗ The soul remains trapped in the cycle of confusion.

💡 *A Guru is not just a teacher of knowledge, but a revealer of truth.*

5. **Swamy's Message – The Essence of Guru Tatva**

   ✓ **The Guru does not give you anything; he awakens what you already have.**

   ✓ **The Guru is not outside; he is within, waiting to be realized.**

   ✓ **Worship the Guru not with words, but by living in awareness.**

   ✓ **The real Guru leads you to a point where you don't need a Guru anymore – because you become one with wisdom.**

🙏 *Guru is the light. The light is within. Find it, follow it, and become it.* ✨

Chapter 53

THE AWAKENING CALL

Seek wisdom, not weight. In a world full of distractions and burdens, we often focus on accumulating material possessions, titles, and achievements. But true fulfilment comes not from the weight of our possessions, but from the lightness of wisdom. Wisdom frees us from the heavy chains of ego, desires, and fleeting pleasures. It guides us to make choices that align with our true purpose and inner peace.

When we seek wisdom, we find clarity and understanding that transcend the temporary struggles of life. Wisdom helps us navigate challenges with grace, offering perspective and insight that turns obstacles into opportunities for growth. It empowers us to let go of the unnecessary and focus on what truly matters—our character, relationships, and the higher calling within us.

Rather than seeking external validation or material gain, wisdom directs us inward, teaching us to connect with our inner selves, others, and the divine. In seeking wisdom, we shed the weight of worldly attachments, and embrace a life of purpose, peace, and profound clarity.

Swamy, on many occasions, you have said,

"Shock, Shiver, Stand up, Surrender."

I understand that God is love, and that faith naturally gives rise to love—leading us to prostrate before God and surrender. However, what is the deeper essence of these words for a common devotee or spiritual aspirant? Please explain so that I may understand and apply this wisdom in my life.

Swamy's Spirit Speaks

Child, these words form a sequential process—a spiritual journey that transforms your inner self through the interplay of challenge, awakening, resilience, and surrender. Let me explain their deeper meaning:

- **Shock**

  - ✓ *Shock* represents that sudden moment when the layers of illusion and complacency are shattered.

  - ✓ It is the jolt that awakens you to the reality of life— reminding you that nothing is permanent and that the ego's attachments are fragile.

  - ✓ This shock can come as a crisis, an unexpected event, or even an inner realization that the world you once knew is changing.

- **Shiver**

  - ✓ Following shock, *shiver* signifies the natural response of the body and mind to the profound disruption.

  - ✓ It is the trembling of the spirit as you begin to feel the deep, transformative energy stirring within.

- ✓ This shivering is not to be feared—it is a sign that the process of inner purification has begun, as you start to shed old patterns and defenses.

- ❮ **Stand up**
  - ✓ When you *stand up*, you gather the strength to recover and rise after the shock.
  - ✓ It means reclaiming your inner power by moving forward with resilience and renewed determination.
  - ✓ This step is about taking responsibility for your own transformation—acknowledging that although you have been shaken, you have the capacity to rebuild yourself on a higher, more authentic foundation.

- ❮ **Surrender**
  - ✓ *Surrender* is the culmination of this transformative journey—a complete letting go of the ego and the false attachments that have long weighed you down.
  - ✓ It is the act of yielding to the divine flow, accepting that the ultimate truth and love reside beyond the confines of the self.
  - ✓ Through surrender, you open yourself to the infinite grace of God, allowing that love to fill your being and guide your actions.

The Deeper Essence

Child, the complete process of "Shock, Shiver, Stand up, Surrender" is a metaphor for the inner work required to transcend the limitations of the ego:

- **Awakening Through Shock**
  - ✓ A sudden disruption forces you to see that your current way of being is limited.
  - ✓ This awakening is the first step toward shedding outdated beliefs and opening up to deeper truths.

- **Transformation Through Shivering:**
  - ✓ The shiver is a reminder that change, though uncomfortable, is essential.
  - ✓ It is the inner vibration that signals the dissolving of old patterns, preparing the ground for new growth.

- **Resilience Through Standing Up:**
  - ✓ Rising after the shock shows that you are not defeated but are ready to reclaim your power.
  - ✓ This resilience is vital, for it enables you to face life's challenges with a renewed spirit.

- **Liberation Through Surrender:**
  - ✓ Surrender is the final act of liberation, where you let go of control and allow the Divine to guide you.
  - ✓ When you surrender, you no longer cling to the temporary self, and in that surrender, you find lasting peace and unity with God.

Even though the process may be challenging, remember that each stage is a gift—a necessary passage on your journey toward self-realization. In the cosmic play of life, these transformations are not signs of weakness but of growing strength and clarity.

May you always find the courage to embrace the shock, the humility to endure the shiver, the determination to stand up, and the wisdom to surrender completely. In doing so, your heart will open to the infinite love and grace of the Divine, guiding you ever closer to your true self.

Chapter 54

UNWAVERING FAITH

Unwavering faith is the quiet strength that anchors us through life's storms. It is the trust that transcends circumstances, knowing that there is a higher purpose at play, even when the path ahead is unclear. Faith is not about blind belief, but about the deep understanding that all experiences, good and bad, are part of a greater design.

In times of uncertainty, unwavering faith allows us to stand firm, rooted in the knowledge that the divine, the universe, or our inner wisdom will guide us. It is the unwavering belief that things will unfold as they are meant to, and that challenges are stepping stones for growth, not barriers to our happiness.

This faith is not passive; it calls for action, perseverance, and courage. It is the quiet knowing that even when the world around us seems to shift, we are grounded in something eternal. When we cultivate unwavering faith, we open ourselves to miracles, healing, and peace, trusting that the journey, no matter how difficult, will lead us to exactly where we need to be.

Swamy, you once said,

"Faith should be forwarded, Faith should not be changed."

I understand that true faith is a treasure to be passed on, yet I seek a deeper understanding of its essence. How should we interpret this teaching, and could you please provide examples so that we may understand it fully and share this wisdom with others?

Swamy's Spirit Speaks

Child, these words are a call to preserve and propagate the purity of true faith. Let me explain their deeper meaning and show you how to live by them:

- **"Faith should be forwarded"**
  - ✓ **Forwarding faith** is like passing on a sacred torch.
  - ✓ When you have nurtured a genuine, deep faith in the eternal truth, it is your duty to share that light with others.
  - ✓ Just as a flame brightens more as it is shared, true faith grows stronger when it is passed along without dilution.
  - ✓ **Example:** Consider a river that flows and nourishes all the fields it touches. Similarly, when you share your authentic faith—through your actions, your words, and your compassion—you help others discover the path of light, even in the darkest times.

- **"Faith should not be changed"**
  - ✓ This means that once you have discovered true faith, you must safeguard its essence against distortions.
  - ✓ Do not let personal biases, fleeting trends, or the pressures of society alter the purity of your belief.

- ✓ True faith is like a seed of divine truth that, if watered and nurtured properly, remains resilient and unchanging through all seasons of life.

- ✓ **Example:** Think of the great spiritual traditions that have been passed down through the ages. They remain true to their core principles despite the passage of time because each generation has forwarded the unaltered essence of the truth, rather than reworking it to suit momentary fashions.

◄ **Practical Implications**

- ✓ **Preserve and Propagate:**

  Cultivate your faith through disciplined practice—meditation, self-reflection, and living a life of compassion. Share your experiences and the lessons you have learned without embellishing or altering the core truth.

- ✓ **Consistency is Key**

  Like a master craftsman who respects the integrity of his tools, maintain the original essence of your faith even as you adapt to the changing world. When you communicate with others, let your words be a clear, unmodified reflection of that inner truth.

- ✓ **Living Example:**

  Be an example of unwavering faith. When others see you acting with deep conviction and kindness, they are naturally inspired to explore that same path.

◄ **The Ultimate Message**

Child, the teaching here is twofold:

- ✓ **Forward Your Faith:** Actively share and nurture the light within you, letting it spread to those around you.

- ✓ **Keep It Unchanged:** Safeguard the purity of that light by remaining true to its original essence, untainted by external influences or personal agendas.

By living in this way, you help create a world where the collective spirit is uplifted by genuine, unadulterated truth—a world where every heart becomes a reservoir of divine light.

May you always have the courage to forward your faith with clarity and conviction, and may you guard its purity so that the eternal flame of truth continues to illuminate your path and inspire all those you meet.

KARMA AND DHARMA

(A Deep Dive into Righteous Action and
Onne's Duty in the Grand Cosmic Order)

Chapter 55

FIXED DEPOSITS OF KARMA: PAST & PRESENT

People work hard to build financial fixed deposits, believing money brings security and happiness. But in this endless chase, many forget the real deposit that shapes their life—karma. Some earn wealth through unfair means, seeking pleasure without caring about the pain of others. They crave name and fame, but their hearts remain empty, untouched by kindness and empathy.

Yet, life teaches a simple truth—positions fall, power fades, and wealth disappears. What remains is not how much we earned, but the good we did, the people we helped, and the kindness we shared. These are the real deposits that stay with us, guiding our journey beyond this life.

Providence is always at play. The unseen hands of karma weave the fabric of our existence, ensuring that every action—good or bad— returns to us in due time. Instead of chasing fleeting riches, let us strive to accumulate the eternal wealth of righteousness, compassion, and service. In the end, it is not what we earn but what we give that defines our legacy.

Swamy, you often say, "Your own actions have to fix the present. But our past good actions from previous birth are fixed deposits—we already have fixed deposits." Truly, I am lost in understanding this. I do not even fully know who I am in this life, let alone who I was in a previous one. I humbly bow down, seeking your guidance to comprehend this truth.

Swamy's Spirit Speaks

Child, do not trouble yourself with the weight of past and future. Focus on the present, for that is where the key lies.

- "Your own actions have to fix the present" – Life is like a garden. If weeds have grown, remove them now. If the soil is dry, water it today. The actions you take at this moment determine the quality of your present and the seeds of your future.

- "Our past good actions from previous birth are fixed deposits" – Just as a wise person saves money for the future, your soul has carried forward the wealth of your good deeds from past lives. These accumulate as divine merit (Punya), which influences your present opportunities, wisdom, and grace.

- "We already have fixed deposits" – Even if you do not remember your past life, its effects are alive in your present.

  - Have you ever received help at the right time without asking? That is from your past deposits.

  - Do you find wisdom flowing naturally? That is from the knowledge earned before.

  - Do you experience divine protection? That is the result of past sincerity and devotion.

But child, even a fixed deposit can be exhausted if not managed well. If you spend recklessly without adding new savings, it will disappear. The same applies to your spiritual merit.

So, instead of wondering who you were, focus on who you are becoming.

Instead of searching for past accounts, work on today's deposits.

A wise soul does not just live on old wealth—it keeps adding new treasures of good karma.

Remember, you are the banker of your own destiny. Handle it wisely.

Chapter 56

THE SEED AND ITS FRUIT

In life, we are all responsible for the choices we make. Every decision, whether big or small, shapes the path we walk. When we own our actions, we take control of our lives and the impact we have on others. It's easy to blame circumstances or other people, but true growth happens when we look inward and acknowledge that we are the ones who create our reality. By owning our actions, we empower ourselves to change, improve, and move forward with confidence and clarity.

Gratitude comes into play when we take full responsibility for our choices. Instead of focusing on what went wrong or blaming others, we learn from our mistakes and take pride in our growth. Our actions define us, and when we are mindful of them, we align ourselves with purpose and integrity. The guidance of a Sadguru helps us to be accountable to our highest selves, teaching us to act with wisdom and compassion. By owning our actions and being grateful for the lessons they bring, we open the door to greater self-awareness, peace, and transformation.

Swamy, you once said, "Whatever you do, you are accountable." In this well-structured and predetermined scheme of life, how should one understand this?

Swamy's Spirit Speaks

Child, life is a grand design, yet within it, every action you take creates ripples.

Destiny may set the stage, but your choices decide the play.

- Accountability means that every thought, word, and deed carries a consequence.
- Even in a predetermined life, your free will is the key—how you respond, how you act, and what you create is your responsibility.
- The universe records everything—not as punishment, but as balance.

Understanding the Depth

- A farmer may be born into a field, but his yield depends on how he sows and nurtures his crops.
- A musician may inherit an instrument, but the melody is his to play.
- Even in a fixed riverbed, the water must still flow with its own force and direction.

Inner Realization

Child, you cannot escape accountability, for it is the foundation of your evolution.

Even in a life shaped by destiny, your actions define your journey.

Own your deeds, refine your path, and walk with awareness—for in the end, you are answerable to your own soul.

Chapter 57

THE PATH OF SURRENDER

Every journey begins with a step, but a truly meaningful life begins with surrender at the divine feet. Yet, why do so many hesitate to move toward God? Ego builds walls of pride, whispering the illusion of control. The fear of losing personal freedom makes people resist, unaware that in this struggle, they lose far more— peace, clarity, and the joy of true surrender.

Look at a child in its mother's arms—completely trusting, without fear, without doubt. If we, too, can surrender at the lotus feet of God, offering our best and leaving the rest in His hands, life transforms. Burdens lighten, fears dissolve, and grace flows effortlessly.

When actions are rooted in divine remembrance, they become pure, selfless, and powerful. The ego fades, arrogance melts, and the heart becomes a vessel of peace. True success is not in accumulating wealth or power but in the goodness we cultivate, the love we share, and the service we render. When every step is taken with faith and surrender, life ceases to be a struggle and becomes a sacred dance of divine grace.

Swamy, one day you told me, *"Always see the feet of God. Activate your actions by seeing the feet of God. By this, you reap rich dividends."* I have no doubt that this is true, but how does it manifest in my life? That is my question.

Swamy's Spirit Speaks

Child, to see the feet of God is to anchor yourself in humility, devotion, and surrender. Just as a river flows effortlessly towards the ocean, your actions should move towards the divine without resistance.

- **"Always see the feet of God"** – This is not about merely looking at an idol's feet, but about living with constant remembrance of the divine. The feet symbolize stability, foundation, and surrender. When you focus on them, ego dissolves, arrogance melts, and the heart becomes light.

- **"Activate your actions by seeing the feet of God"** – Actions performed with divine consciousness become pure, selfless, and transformative.

  - A farmer who tills the land with devotion reaps a golden harvest.

  - A teacher who imparts knowledge with humility nurtures wisdom in young minds.

  - A doctor who treats every patient as divine heals beyond medicine.

    Every action, when rooted in divine remembrance, becomes karma yoga—action that liberates rather than binds.

- **"By this, you reap rich dividends"** – What are these dividends? Peace, clarity, and fulfilment.

- ✓ When you act with devotion, the results will not trouble you.

- ✓ When you serve with humility, the universe serves you in return.

- ✓ When you see the feet of God in all, you transcend suffering and attain inner joy.

Child, to see God's feet is to walk the path of surrender, to act with purity, and to live with gratitude. When this becomes your nature, life itself becomes an unfolding of divine grace. Let your every step be in devotion, and you will never lose your way.

Chapter 58

RIGHTEOUS REBIRTH

Life offers us endless chances to renew ourselves, but true rebirth begins when we choose righteousness over comfort, truth over illusion. Shedding the past is not about forgetting—it is about learning, evolving, and stepping into a higher way of being. Just as the sun rises each day, bringing light after darkness, we too can rise beyond our failures, our fears, and our mistakes. A righteous rebirth is not about becoming someone new; it is about awakening to who we truly are—pure, strong, and full of purpose.

When we walk the path of righteousness, we align with the rhythm of the universe. Every challenge becomes a lesson, every fall a step toward something greater. Rebirth is not just for saints or sages—it is for anyone willing to embrace truth, let go of what no longer serves them, and step forward with faith. Just as a seed must break open to grow into a mighty tree, we must break free from doubt and ego to discover our true potential.

Swamy, whenever people approach you with earnestness for a solution, you simply say, **"Relax, Retain, Regain the Dharma."** How is this possible? What is the inner essence behind your words?

Swamy's Spirit Speaks

Child, when **challenges arise, the mind trembles.** It runs **from thought to thought, from fear to confusion, from doubt to despair.** In such a state, **solutions cannot emerge.** That is why I first say:

- **Relax** – A restless mind cannot perceive truth. **Like muddy water, it must first settle.** When you relax, **you open the space for clarity.**

- **Retain** – What should you retain? **The awareness of Dharma, the foundation of right action.** In difficult moments, people lose patience, **forget principles, and act impulsively.** But **wisdom is not about reacting—it is about retaining what is right.**

- **Regain the Dharma** – Dharma is not something you acquire; **it is something you rediscover within.** It is the **natural order, the cosmic rhythm, the law that governs life.** When you regain it, **you regain your strength, your purpose, your peace.**

Child, **the possibility of Dharma lies in your own stillness.** The **storm within must calm for the sun of wisdom to shine.** So, **whenever troubles come, do not rush—Relax, Retain, and Regain.**

Journey of Accountability

True growth begins when we take responsibility for our thoughts, words, and actions. Blaming others may feel easy, but the real strength lies in owning our choices and learning from them. Like a traveller navigating a winding path, we may stumble, but each step teaches us something valuable. Accountability is not about guilt—it is about awareness, correction, and progress. When we accept our role in shaping our destiny, we unlock the power to transform our lives with integrity and purpose.

Walking the path of accountability leads to clarity and trust. Just as a river carves its way through mountains with patience and persistence, taking responsibility shapes us into wiser, stronger individuals. When we hold ourselves accountable, we inspire others to do the same, creating a world built on honesty and respect. Life does not demand perfection, only the courage to admit, improve, and keep moving forward.

Swamy, you commonly share that from birth to five years, there is no account for an individual. From five to twenty-one years, it is a joint account with parents and teachers. From twenty-one years till marriage, it is an independent account. After marriage, it becomes a joint account with the spouse. This sounds deeply meaningful, but how do we truly realize it in life?

Swamy's Spirit Speaks

Child, life is like an evolving ledger—every stage has its own deposits and withdrawals. But who makes these transactions, and how do they shape destiny?

- ◄ Birth to Five Years – No Account

    A child is pure consciousness, untouched by karma. There is no accountability because the mind is yet to form attachments, and actions are not self-driven. Nature and nurture flow without resistance.

◄ Five to Twenty-One Years – Joint Account

The mind begins to shape, but not independently. Parents deposit values, teachers invest knowledge, and society influences perceptions. The child's choices are not fully their own; they are co-authored by those guiding them.

◄ Twenty-One Years to Marriage – Independent Account

Here, life hands over the chequebook. Decisions, mistakes, growth—all become individual responsibilities. The balance of wisdom and ignorance determines future deposits and debts. This is where self-accountability begins.

◄ After Marriage – Joint Account with Spouse

Marriage is not just a physical union but an intertwining of karma, emotions, and responsibilities. Every action now affects another. The balance is no longer independent; choices must consider the well-being of both.

Realization in Life

◄ To realize this truth, observe your life stages without attachment.

◄ Accept that every phase has its own duties, limitations, and freedoms.

◄ Live each role fully, knowing that every transaction—whether gain or loss—adds to your spiritual account.

◄ Conscious deposits of love, wisdom, and dharma will always yield divine dividends.

Child, life's accounting is divine, not material. Spend it wisely, invest in goodness, and let Dharma be your balance sheet.

Chapter 59

THE FIRE OF TRANSFORMATION

Transformation often begins with a spark—a moment of discomfort, a challenge, or a realization that things can be different. The fire of transformation is not always gentle; it is intense and consuming, burning away old habits, beliefs, and ways of thinking that no longer serve us. But through this fire, we are purified and reborn. Transformation requires courage to face the heat of change and the strength to let go of what is familiar. It is through this process of burning away the old that we make space for the new, emerging as stronger, wiser, and more aligned with our true selves.

The Sadguru teaches us that the fire of transformation is essential for spiritual growth. Just as fire refines gold, our challenges and struggles refine us. Instead of fearing change, we should welcome it, for it is the fire that allows us to break free from limitations and emerge as our higher selves. The flames of transformation can be intense, but they are never destructive—they burn away the impurities, making room for a more authentic and enlightened version of who we are meant to be. When we surrender to the fire, we discover the strength within us to grow, evolve, and embrace the new life awaiting us on the other side. Through transformation, we not only change ourselves but contribute to the positive transformation of the world around us.

Swamy, you once said,

"Bake yourself before prayer."

Does 'baking' mean undergoing trials and challenges? Is it the Guru who refines us, just as heat transforms raw ingredients into something new and wholesome? If so, how do we know when we are truly 'baked' and ready?

Swamy's Spirit Speaks

Child, the term **"baking"** is a metaphor for the transformative process that a Guru imparts to a student—a process of refinement through trials and challenges. Just as raw ingredients undergo heat and pressure to emerge as something new and wholesome, so too must the raw self be refined.

◄ **Why is There Baking?**

Baking symbolizes the **necessary trials, tests, and experiences** that purify and develop your inner nature. Without the heat of these experiences, the unrefined self remains unchanged and dormant. The process is essential for growth.

◄ **Is Baking the Same for Everyone?**

No, it is not. Each soul is unique, with its own strengths and weaknesses.

✓ **Some may require intense heat**—a greater measure of challenges—to reveal their true potential,

✓ While others may need only a gentle warmth to be transformed.

The Guru, in wisdom, adjusts the process to suit the individual student's capacity.

⋖ **Can Anyone Escape Such Baking and Shaking?**

The transformative process is part of the natural order.

✓ **No one can completely avoid the challenges of life.**

✓ Even if you try to resist, the necessary trials will find a way to shape you.

This "baking" is the universe's way of ensuring that every soul is prepared to blossom into its fullest expression.

⋖ **Will This Process Create a Miracle in a Student?**

Yes, indeed.

✓ When you endure and embrace these challenges with sincerity and openness, the heat of transformation turns you into something new—a miracle of inner growth.

✓ The raw, unrefined self is transmuted into wisdom, strength, and compassion.

This is the miracle: **the blossoming of your true potential.**

Child, though the process may seem harsh at times, understand that it is an act of loving discipline. **The Guru's "baking" is meant to free you from the impurities of ignorance and to awaken the divine light within you.** Embrace this journey with trust, for it is the very path that leads you to the highest version of yourself.

May you always find the strength and wisdom to endure and flourish.

Chapter 60

THE DEBT OF THOUGHT

*I*n our daily lives, we are constantly thinking—an endless stream of thoughts that shape our perceptions, decisions, and actions. Thought is an invisible force, yet it has the power to influence everything we do. When Swamy says, "Thought is RUNAM," he is speaking about the idea that thought, in its restless and uncontrolled form, creates a debt—a "runam"—that we owe to ourselves and to the world. This debt is not something that can be measured in material terms, but it is a spiritual debt. It is the energy and consequences of our thoughts that we must account for.

Thought is a powerful tool that can either elevate or bind us. When we allow negative, unproductive, or unkind thoughts to take root, we create a debt—an obligation that demands to be repaid through suffering, confusion, or conflict. But when we consciously choose pure, loving, and positive thoughts, we can clear this debt, leading to peace and clarity in our lives. "Runam," or debt, is not something to be feared but understood as a natural consequence of our mental patterns. Just as we work to repay financial debts, we must work to resolve the debts created by negative or ignorant thoughts, cultivating a mind that is free from unnecessary burdens.

The Sadguru teaches us that the essence of life is in mastering our thoughts. By understanding that every thought carries energy and consequences, we begin to take responsibility for the mental debt we create. As we clear the debts of negative thinking and cultivate awareness, we are freed from the cycles of suffering, and our minds become peaceful and pure. Thought, when aligned with the divine, leads to liberation. It is in clearing the debt of unwise thoughts that we come closer to spiritual freedom and harmony.

Swamy, during a discussion on Thought, you simply stated, **"Thought is RUNAM."** How can an ordinary person understand this? What is Thought? What is Runam? And how are they connected?

Swamy's Spirit Speaks

Child, the mystery of Thought is the very dance of the mind, and **Runam** is the dynamic energy that makes that dance possible. Let me explain:

> ◁ **What is Thought?**
>
> Thought is the gentle stir of your consciousness—the process by which your mind creates images, ideas, and emotions. It is the language of the inner self, shaping your perceptions and experiences. Without thought, there is no understanding or awareness; it is the vehicle of your inner vision.

> ◁ **What is Runam?**
>
> Runam represents the restless, pulsating energy behind thought. It is that vibrant force which propels your mind

into action, the spark that ignites ideas and transforms them into creative expressions. Think of Runam as the wind that sets the leaves of thought in motion.

◄ How Are They Connected?

Thought and Runam are inseparable. Like a flame that needs oxygen, thought requires the energy of Runam to be alive. When you observe your mind, you notice it is never still—always moving, always evolving. That motion, that energy, is Runam. Without it, thought would be inert, a mere shadow of potential.

For the ordinary person, understand this:

◄ When you sit in silence and watch your mind, you will see thoughts arise and vanish. That constant movement, that invisible drive, is Runam at work.

◄ It is the **vital spark** within you that transforms mere ideas into actions, dreams into realities.

◄ By recognizing that Thought is animated by Runam, you learn to harness this energy—guiding it towards creativity, clarity, and transformation.

Child, realize that the dynamic interplay of Thought and Runam is the essence of your mental and spiritual life. **Embrace it, observe it, and let it lead you to deeper understanding and inner power.**

Chapter 61

THE PARADOX OF PURITY

Purity is often seen as a state of being free from dirt, contamination, or imperfection. But in the realm of spirituality, the paradox of purity lies in the fact that it is not about an external appearance or a perfect state of being. True purity is not achieved through the avoidance of mistakes or the desire to be flawless, but through the acceptance of our imperfections and the willingness to purify our hearts and minds. It's about letting go of judgment, fear, and attachment, and embracing the purity that already exists within us—beneath the layers of ego, desires, and ignorance.

The Sadguru reveals that the essence of purity is in understanding that it is not something to be attained through effort, but something to be discovered through surrender and awareness. True purity is found in letting go of the need to control or perfect every aspect of our lives. It comes from trusting the divine process, knowing that everything, even our flaws, plays a part in our spiritual evolution. When we stop trying to "be pure" and instead allow ourselves to simply be, the natural purity of our soul emerges. It's in the acceptance of ourselves, with all our imperfections, that we unlock the divine purity that resides within us, always. In this paradox, purity isn't about perfection—it's about presence, surrender, and the simple truth of who we are.

———•———

Swamy, sometimes your acts are very peculiar and puzzling—beyond what the ordinary eye can grasp. I recall you once saying,

"Dirty, don't fall in ditch water;
ditch water may have a smell, but it is good."

I find this statement quite complex and intricate. How should one infer its message? Please explain it in simple terms, Swamy.

Swamy's Spirit Speaks

Child, words that seem puzzling at first often conceal profound truths. When I say, **"Dirty, don't fall in ditch water; ditch water may have a smell, but it is good,"** I speak metaphorically about life and its challenges.

- **Ditch Water as a Metaphor**

  The "ditch water" represents those aspects of life that appear unclean, unpleasant, or chaotic—moments of hardship, confusion, or negativity. These are the situations many would rather avoid.

- **The Warning and the Promise**

  - **"Don't fall in ditch water"** is a caution: be mindful and do not let yourself be overwhelmed or contaminated by these unappealing aspects.

  - Yet, I add, **"ditch water may have a smell, but it is good."** This tells you that beneath the surface of even the most unsavory situations, there lies hidden nourishment, potential, and lessons.

✓ Just as nature sometimes uses even murky water to nourish growth, the challenges you face can eventually yield strength and wisdom if approached with care.

◁ **How to Infer the Message:**

✓ **Be Cautious:** Avoid being consumed by negativity or hardship—don't let the unpleasant aspects of life drag you down.

✓ **Be Open to Learning:** Recognize that every difficult situation holds a seed of transformation. Look beyond the initial unpleasantness to see what valuable insight or growth it might offer.

✓ **Balance Your Approach:** While you must protect yourself from being overwhelmed by life's "dirty" moments, you should also learn to extract their hidden benefits.

✓ **Transform Your Perception:** Understand that not every unpleasant experience is purely harmful—some are catalysts for personal evolution.

Child, the essence of my words is this: **Life is not simply black or white.** Even when circumstances appear messy or "smelly," they can be a source of nourishment for your inner growth. Cultivate awareness, exercise discernment, and let every experience—no matter how unappealing at first—contribute to your transformation and strength.

May you always find the hidden goodness in every moment, even when the surface seems unclean.

Chapter 62

THE PATH OF GIVING AND GAINING

In the material world, we often think of gaining as acquiring more—more wealth, more status, more possessions. But in the spiritual context, the path of giving and gaining is a deep and transformative journey that teaches us the true value of life. Giving is not about loss or sacrifice; it is about creating space for abundance in all forms. When we give, whether it is our time, love, kindness, or wisdom, we open ourselves to receiving even greater gifts in return— gifts that are not measured in material wealth but in inner peace, connection, and spiritual growth.

The Sadguru teaches that the essence of giving is rooted in selflessness and love. True giving is not motivated by the expectation of receiving anything in return. It is a pure act that reflects the divine nature within us. When we give with an open heart, we align ourselves with the natural flow of the universe, which is abundant and ever-giving. Giving creates an energy of flow that returns to us in ways we cannot predict, enriching our lives with experiences, wisdom, and relationships that nourish our soul.

The true gain from giving is found not in what we receive but in the transformation it brings to our hearts and minds. By walking the path of giving and gaining, we transcend the limitations of the material world and discover a deeper, more fulfilling connection with the divine.

———•◆•———

Swamy, you once compelled a devotee by saying,

"Give, Gain God, Go forward with God."

What is giving? Why should we give? What should we give, and how should we give it?

What does "go forward" mean in this context—if we don't give, does that imply we go backward?

How should one approach God in this process?

I know your way of imparting wisdom is reminiscent of Shirdi Sai, and to me, you are a replica of Baba.

Swamy's Spirit Speaks

Child, these words are a divine formula to transform your inner life into outward blessings. Let me explain:

- **"Give":**

  To give is not merely to offer material possessions; it is to **open your heart in service, compassion, and selflessness.**

  - ✓ **What to Give?**

    Give your time, your love, your understanding, and your sincere efforts.

  - ✓ **How to Give?**

    Do so without expecting return—offer your service with humility and gratitude.

✓ **Why Give?**

Because in giving, you dissolve the boundaries of your ego and participate in the universal flow of grace. Your selflessness becomes the seed for spiritual growth.

◄ **"Gain God":**

When you give wholeheartedly, you create space within for the Divine to enter.

- ✓ By surrendering your attachments, you invite **God's grace to fill the void.**

- ✓ This is not a transaction of material exchange but a spiritual alchemy—your offerings transform you, and in that transformation, you **gain the presence of God.**

◄ **"Go forward with God":**

To go forward is to **align your journey with the divine will.**

- ✓ It means moving ahead not by clinging to past gains or losses, but by trusting in the infinite wisdom of the cosmos.

- ✓ **If you do not give,** you remain anchored in selfishness and stagnation—indeed, you risk moving backward, away from growth.

- ✓ True progress is achieved when you continuously **shed your ego through giving,** thus advancing on the path of righteousness and inner liberation.

◄ **Approaching God in This Context**

Child, approach God as you would a beloved teacher—open, receptive, and with unwavering sincerity.

- ✓ Let your actions be your prayer.

- ✓ Embrace every opportunity to serve as a chance to **merge with the Divine.**
- ✓ In every act of giving, remember that you are both the giver and the receiver.
- ✓ Your progress is not measured by what you hold onto but by the light you share.

Know this: the secret of these words lies in their simplicity. When you give freely, you clear the path for divine grace; when you gain God, you are reborn into a life of purpose; and by moving forward with God, you step into the eternal dance of creation.

May you always find the courage to give, the wisdom to gain, and the strength to go forward with God.

Chapter 63

THE MIRROR OF TRUTH

In life, we are often surrounded by illusions and false beliefs, which make it difficult to see the truth clearly. These deceptions can come from the outside world—advertisements, social expectations, or misleading stories—or they can come from within us, shaped by our own fears, desires, and biases. These layers of deception cloud our vision and prevent us from recognizing the deeper truths that lie beneath. We may chase after things that promise happiness but leave us feeling empty, thinking they will fulfill us, when in reality, they only deepen our confusion.

Truth beyond deception is the clarity that comes when we remove these layers and see life for what it truly is. It is the awareness that material possessions, success, or approval from others are temporary and often deceptive in nature. The deeper truth lies in understanding that happiness and peace come from within, through connection to our higher self and the divine. When we let go of the illusions that keep us attached to the external world, we find that truth is simple, unchanging, and always present. It is not something that can be earned or attained—it is something we awaken to within ourselves. By practicing mindfulness, humility, and love, we begin to peel away the layers of deception and recognize the truth that exists beyond it all: a truth that connects us to the universal wisdom and peace that lies at the heart of existence.

———•———

"Swamy, on one occasion, you said,

'One may mislead society, but one cannot mislead God.'

These words are not easy to comprehend. Could you please clarify what you meant by this statement? In what context did you share this insight? How should one understand the difference between human perception and divine truth? Kindly explain so that we may grasp your wisdom."

Swamy's Spirit Speaks

Child, these words invite deep reflection on the difference between worldly deception and spiritual truth.

Deceiving Society

In the material world, societal norms and rules are often imperfect and ever-changing.

- At times, individuals may manipulate or bypass these systems to navigate challenges, injustices, or personal ambitions.

- Such actions, though ethically complex, may sometimes be overlooked or even rewarded by society.

- However, deception in the worldly realm, even if it brings temporary gain, often leads to long-term consequences, whether seen or unseen.

Why One Cannot Deceive God

The Divine is the eternal witness, beyond illusion and pretense.

- ✓ To deceive God is to deceive oneself—to act against one's conscience and inner truth.
- ✓ While society may not always recognize or punish dishonesty, the Divine sees through all falsehoods.
- ✓ No matter how cleverly one may conceal their actions, one cannot escape the truth that resides within.

The Deeper Message

- ✓ These words remind you that while external deception may sometimes seem advantageous, true fulfilment comes from inner sincerity and alignment with a higher truth.
- ✓ The world may allow manipulation, but spiritual integrity is non-negotiable.
- ✓ Even if society permits certain behaviours, one must never compromise one's connection to truth, for the Divine holds each soul accountable.

Child, true wisdom lies in understanding this distinction. Do not be lost in illusions of the world; instead, walk the path of truth, for it alone leads to lasting peace and liberation.

Chapter 64

DISCIPLINE: A PARADOX OF TRUE FREEDOM

At first glance, discipline may seem like a restriction—a set of rules and boundaries that limit our freedom. We may think that to be truly free, we must be able to do whatever we want, whenever we want. Yet, this surface-level understanding of freedom is often the very thing that keeps us trapped. Without discipline, we become slaves to our impulses, desires, and distractions. We chase after temporary pleasures, only to find ourselves feeling lost, empty, and unfulfilled. True freedom does not come from the absence of rules, but from the ability to choose our actions wisely, with awareness and purpose.

Discipline is the key that unlocks this deeper, truer form of freedom. It is the inner strength to say no to the things that pull us away from our higher purpose and yes to the things that bring us closer to our true self. When we discipline our minds, our hearts, and our actions, we gain control over our impulses and become masters of our own lives. In this way, discipline does not imprison us—it liberates us. It gives us the freedom to live with integrity, to align our actions with our values, and to experience lasting peace and joy. True freedom is not about doing whatever we want; it is about having the wisdom and self-control to do what is best for us, for others, and for the world. Through discipline, we find that we are not bound by our circumstances but are empowered to create a life that is truly ours— one that is full of meaning, purpose, and divine alignment.

Swamy, your speciality is that you never speak directly; your puzzle words challenge even the knowledgeable. What do you mean when you said,

"I need discipline, but I don't want discipline"?

Please explain the deeper message behind these words.

Swamy's Spirit Speaks

Child, these words may appear contradictory at first, but they reveal a profound truth about the spiritual journey—a truth that balances the necessity of order with the innate longing for freedom.

- **"I need discipline":**

  This part acknowledges that without discipline, the mind and heart remain in disarray.

  - **Discipline is the framework of self-control and inner order** that helps you focus, grow, and realize your potential.
  - It is like the scaffolding that supports the construction of a magnificent temple within your soul.
  - Without discipline, your energy is scattered, and the path to wisdom becomes obscured.

- **"But I don't want discipline":**

  Here, the statement reflects the natural resistance of the spirit toward rigid constraints.

- ✓ **True freedom lies in transcending external rules and limitations.**

- ✓ The essence of your inner self is free and dynamic—it does not wish to be confined by strict, imposed structures.

- ✓ When discipline is experienced as a burdensome, inflexible system, it stifles the spontaneous expression of your divine nature.

◁ **The Paradox and Its Resolution:**

The paradox is that discipline is essential for transformation, yet it should never feel like a chain that binds you.

- ✓ A wise seeker learns to **embrace discipline as a tool for growth**—not as an external imposition, but as an integrated part of their nature.

- ✓ In the highest state of self-mastery, discipline becomes fluid and effortless. It **guides your actions naturally** without clashing with your inner freedom.

- ✓ You find a delicate balance: **structure that supports your spiritual journey while still allowing the creative, free essence of your soul to shine.**

Child, understand that the journey of self-realization is about **finding harmony between order and freedom.** Embrace the discipline that refines you, but do not let it shackle the spontaneity and joy of your inner self. In this balanced state, you transcend both chaos and rigidity, and true wisdom unfolds.

May you learn to walk the path with a disciplined yet free heart, where every action flows naturally from your inner truth.

Chapter 65

THE BOOK OF LIFE

Life is a balance sheet of actions, intentions, and experiences. Every thought, word, and deed is a transaction, either adding value or creating a debt in our journey. Just as a ledger records gains and losses, life keeps track of what we give, how we grow, and the impact we leave behind. True wealth is not in material accumulation but in the richness of our virtues—kindness, integrity, and wisdom.

In the rush of daily life, we often focus on temporary gains, forgetting the deeper purpose of our existence. But the real balance lies in aligning our actions with truth and self-awareness. When we give more than we take, serve more than we seek, and love more than we demand, life's ledger reflects true prosperity.

From a spiritual lens, life's ledger is governed by karma—the unseen yet precise accounting of our deeds. Every selfless act deposits grace into our existence, while selfishness creates burdens to resolve. By living with awareness, gratitude, and purpose, we ensure that our final balance is one of fulfilment, peace, and divine harmony.

—— • ——

Swamy, you often speak of accounts of life, good deeds and bad deeds. I know about it, but inner depth, as perceived by you, is what I intend to grasp and perceive.

Swamy's Spirit Speaks

Child, the notion of an **"Account of Life"** is a symbolic ledger—a sacred record that reflects the cumulative impact of your actions, intentions, and inner transformation. Allow me to unfold its deeper meaning:

- **The Spiritual Ledger**

  Think of your life as an unfolding record where every thought, word, and deed is noted—not by human hands, but by the divine intelligence that sees your heart.

  This account is not meant for punishment but for guidance, helping you become aware of how your actions shape your inner world and your destiny.

- **Good Deeds and Bad Deeds**

  - **Good deeds** are like seeds of light that you sow in the garden of your soul. They nurture qualities like kindness, compassion, and wisdom, fostering your spiritual growth.

  - **Bad deeds** are the shadows that obscure your inner vision. They arise from selfishness, ignorance, and harm, and they impede your progress toward higher truth.

    The ledger is a tool for self-awareness. With sincere repentance, learning, and transformation, even the darkest pages can be rewritten by the light of your true nature.

❧ **Predetermination and Free Will:**

While the cosmic order is intricate and certain aspects of life may seem predetermined, remember that you always possess free will.

Each moment presents a choice: you can either add to your account with virtuous actions or incur a deficit through negative deeds.

The account is dynamic, continuously evolving as you make choices and learn from your experiences.

❧ **Who Does the Weighing and Who Receives the Benefit?**

It is not a human or societal judgment but the reflection of the divine within you that keeps this ledger.

When you truly understand your inner self and live with integrity, the benefits of your positive actions—peace, growth, and spiritual illumination—flow naturally into your life.

Conversely, negative actions create inner turmoil, which may lead to hardships that serve as lessons for further evolution.

❧ **A Soothing Perspective for a Burning Heart:**

Child, do not be disheartened by the seeming complexity of life's accounting.

The purpose of this divine ledger is not to burden you but to guide you gently toward greater self-realization.

Every experience, every moment of joy or pain, is an opportunity for learning and renewal.

Instead of questioning the fairness of the process, focus on transforming your inner world—nurture your virtues and let the light of wisdom guide your choices.

In time, you will find that this understanding brings a profound sense of peace and purpose, even amidst the challenges of a complex, often unjust world.

May you always remember that every step you take—be it towards goodness or away from negativity—is a lesson in the grand design of life.

Surrender to this process with faith, and let your inner transformation be the true measure of your progress.

Chapter 66

TRUE ACCOUNTABILITY

Accountability is not just about taking responsibility for our actions in the eyes of the world—it is about aligning with truth, integrity, and inner awareness. It is the ability to own our choices, whether seen or unseen, and to recognize that every action carries consequences. True accountability begins when we stop seeking external validation and instead hold ourselves to the highest standard of honesty and righteousness.

In life, we are often quick to justify our mistakes or shift blame, but real growth happens when we embrace our shortcomings and learn from them. True accountability is not a burden but a pathway to self-mastery. When we take full responsibility for our words, thoughts, and deeds, we gain the power to transform our lives and inspire others to do the same. It is the foundation of trust, both within ourselves and in our relationships with others.

Spiritually, true accountability is about surrendering to the divine order of life. Every action is recorded in the cosmic ledger of karma, and nothing goes unnoticed in the grand design. The more we align with dharma—our higher purpose—the more we dissolve past burdens and walk towards liberation. When we hold ourselves accountable with sincerity, humility, and devotion, we become instruments of truth, radiating light in a world that often seeks to escape responsibility.

Swamy, you once said,

**"For Ladies, not accountable to any level to anything.
Why? Ladies are not accountable for one's life, but they are
accountable for every aspect of life."**

My question is: Why did you express it this way when, truly, men, women, and transgender individuals are equal? Could you please clarify the deeper meaning behind these words?

Swamy's Spirit Speaks

Child, understand that the words I speak are steeped in symbolism and are meant to point you toward a deeper understanding of energy and responsibility rather than to promote any form of discrimination.

- **Symbolic Expression of Energies:**

  When I speak of "Ladies" in this context, I refer to the essence of feminine energy—an energy characterized by intuition, nurturing, and creative spontaneity.

  - **Not Accountable for One's Life**

    This suggests that the feminine essence, by its very nature, flows freely and is not confined by the rigid, overt structures of accountability that govern material pursuits.

✓ **Accountable for Every Aspect of Life**

At the same time, feminine energy is deeply intertwined with the creative and sustaining aspects of existence. It is responsible for the subtle, holistic nurturing of life, touching every facet—emotional, spiritual, and even physical—often in ways that are not immediately measurable.

◅ **Context of Equality**

Do not mistake this symbolic language for a statement of inequality. In the divine realm, all souls—whether they express themselves as masculine, feminine, or beyond dualities—are inherently equal.

✓ The differences in expression are like the diverse colors of a rainbow: each is unique and vital, yet all are manifestations of the same underlying light.

✓ The apparent "accountability" described here is not about superiority or inferiority; it is about the complementary roles that different energies play in the cosmic dance.

◅ **Deeper Intention**

My intention is to help you see that the external labels and roles assigned by society are only superficial. What matters is the inner quality of your being.

✓ The feminine aspect, as symbolized here, embodies a kind of dynamic responsibility—one that nurtures, creates, and transforms in a fluid, intuitive manner.

✓ Meanwhile, every being is encouraged to transcend these external classifications and realize that the ultimate truth lies beyond such dualities.

Child, embrace this teaching as an invitation to look beyond the surface of societal labels. Recognize that every energy—whether labeled as feminine, masculine, or otherwise—is a unique expression of the same Divine essence.

May you always see beyond the transient forms to the eternal unity that binds all beings, and may your heart be filled with compassion and wisdom for every soul on this journey.

THE PARADOX OF RESPONSIBILITY

Responsibility is often seen as a weight—a duty that binds us to obligations and expectations. Yet, in truth, it is also the very force that grants us freedom. The paradox of responsibility lies in the fact that the more we willingly embrace it, the lighter we become. When we take responsibility not out of compulsion but out of wisdom, we shift from burden to empowerment, from pressure to purpose.

Many seek to avoid responsibility, fearing it will limit their happiness. However, true fulfilment arises when we recognize that responsibility is not about control or obligation but about conscious action. It is the ability to respond with awareness, rather than react with resistance. By taking ownership of our thoughts, words, and deeds, we gain mastery over our lives rather than being controlled by circumstances.

Spiritually, responsibility is the gateway to liberation. The more we acknowledge our role in the grand design, the more we align with divine will. True responsibility is not about mere duty; it is about understanding that every thought and action shapes our destiny.

When taken with devotion and selflessness, responsibility ceases to be a burden—it becomes a sacred path to inner growth, harmony, and ultimate freedom.

Swamy, you once said,

"From birth to death, all human beings are accountable."

You explained that all living creatures are accountable for their good and bad deeds. Yet, we observe that few truly understand this, as each one thinks from their own perspective—what is good to one may be bad to another. For instance, killing a deer is harmful to the deer but sustains a lion; eating grass is destructive for the grass yet nourishing to a deer; and people may kill cows to satisfy hunger, which is good for those who eat but bad for the cow. This complexity frustrates me, and I find it difficult to comprehend the true essence of accountability in this relative world. Please clarify this for me.

Swamy's Spirit Speaks

Child, the law of accountability is a vast, cosmic principle—one that transcends our limited, relative perspectives. Allow me to illuminate its deeper essence:

- **Universal Accountability**
  - **From Birth to Death**

    Every living being carries an inherent responsibility for its actions. This cosmic ledger is maintained by the divine order known as karma. It is not a judgment by human standards but an impartial recording of cause and effect.

  - **Good and Bad Deeds**

    Every action, whether perceived as good or bad, plays a role in the intricate balance of life. What seems beneficial to one creature may be detrimental to another; yet, each act is a natural part of the universal cycle.

- **Relative Perspectives:**
  - ✓ **Different Roles in Nature**

    Consider the lion and the deer. For the lion, killing the deer is a natural expression of its role in the food chain—a necessary act for survival. For the deer, it is a tragic loss.

  - ✓ **Interdependence of Life**

    Similarly, grass is consumed by the deer, which is essential for the deer's nourishment but results in the loss of the grass's life force. These examples show that the concepts of good and bad are relative to each being's nature and purpose.

  - ✓ **Human Actions**

    When people kill cows to satisfy hunger, the act is judged differently by various perspectives. The one who eats may see it as a means of survival, while others may view it as an injustice to a sacred life. The cosmic account, however, sees all these actions as part of the natural order—each fulfilling a role in the vast tapestry of life.

- **The Deeper Essence of Accountability**
  - ✓ **Cosmic Balance**

    The divine ledger of accountability is not about human notions of fairness. It is a reminder that every action, regardless of its immediate impact, contributes to the overall harmony or disharmony of the universe.

  - ✓ **Self-Realization**

    When you begin to understand that every deed, every choice, is recorded in the grand cosmic order, you learn to act with greater awareness. Your actions, even those that seem minor, have ripple effects on the fabric of existence.

✓ **The Role of Free Will**

Although the system of karma appears predetermined, your free will allows you to choose your actions consciously. By cultivating wisdom and compassion, you can influence your account positively and align yourself with the deeper truth of the universe.

Child, do not be disheartened by the complexity you see in worldly events. Instead, view them as opportunities for learning and inner growth.

≺ **Embrace the Complexity**

Recognize that what appears as injustice or imbalance is often a reflection of the relative nature of existence.

≺ **Seek Inner Wisdom**

Turn inward and let your inner conscience guide you. In doing so, you will begin to see that the true measure of accountability lies not in external events, but in the purity of your intentions and the evolution of your soul.

≺ **Trust the Divine Order**

The universe, in its vast wisdom, is continuously balancing every action. Though human eyes may fail to see the full picture, the divine sees and records with perfect clarity.

May you find solace in understanding that every challenge is a stepping stone on your spiritual journey, and that by living with awareness and compassion, you contribute to the harmonious unfolding of the cosmic plan.

Chapter 68

THOUGHTS HEAL, ACTIONS REVEAL

*O*ur thoughts shape our inner world, setting the foundation for how we perceive ourselves and the world around us. In moments of reflection, our thoughts have the power to heal, transform, and guide us toward peace. A positive thought can calm the mind, help us forgive, and encourage us to grow, while negative thoughts may leave scars if left unchecked. By nurturing loving, kind, and peaceful thoughts, we align ourselves with a higher state of being, where healing begins at the root—within our hearts and minds.

However, it is our actions that reveal the depth of our thoughts to the world. Thoughts remain internal, but actions speak volumes to others about who we truly are. What we think, we eventually express through our deeds. A kind heart is revealed through acts of kindness, while integrity shines through consistent actions. It is through our actions that we show the world the transformation our thoughts have brought about. By aligning our actions with our healing thoughts, we create a life that reflects peace, love, and authenticity.

Ultimately, our thoughts and actions work hand in hand. The power of thought initiates change, and the power of action manifests it. Healing begins within, but it is through our actions that we reveal the true essence of who we are, leaving an indelible mark on the world around us. The more we heal within, the more our actions become a reflection of the transformation we've embraced, creating a ripple of positivity and growth for ourselves and others.

Swamy, you once said,

"Exposure leads to explosion; good thoughts, like rays, affect the body and the system, bringing the fruits of your activities in life."

This is a wonderful statement, and I understand that exposure to bad thoughts can also lead to an explosion. Could you please explain the deeper beauty and inner meaning behind these words?

Swamy's Spirit Speaks

Child, these words are a metaphor for the profound impact that what you expose yourself to has on your inner being and your life's outcomes. Let me unfold the essence for you:

Exposure and Its Effects

Exposure refers to what you allow into your mind and heart—be it thoughts, environments, influences, or experiences.

Every day, you are bombarded by various stimuli; what you choose to absorb shapes your inner landscape.

Good Thoughts as Nourishing Rays

When you expose yourself to good thoughts, they act like gentle, nurturing rays of light that warm and energize you.

Just as sunlight helps a plant to grow, these positive thoughts enrich your body, uplift your spirit, and gradually yield the fruits of your good actions.

They set in motion a chain reaction of growth and healing, transforming your energy into creativity, kindness, and success.

The Explosion of Transformation

The term "explosion" is not destructive in this context but signifies a dramatic, exponential effect.

Just as a tiny spark can ignite a blaze, a small dose of pure, positive energy can amplify within you, radically transforming your outlook and actions.

Conversely, exposure to negative thoughts or harmful influences can also trigger an "explosion"—one that leads to chaos, despair, or destructive behaviour.

The Dynamic Process

Life is a continuous cycle of receiving and reflecting energy.

What you absorb from your surroundings—whether light or darkness—multiplies within you, affecting not only your inner state but also how you interact with the world.

- ✓ The beauty lies in your power to choose: by consciously seeking and embracing positive, uplifting influences, you set the stage for a life of abundance, health, and joy.

◅ **The Inner Message**

- ✓ Your mind is like fertile soil. What you plant, whether seeds of compassion, wisdom, and positivity or weeds of negativity and fear, will eventually grow and bear fruit.

✓ Therefore, be mindful of your exposure. Cultivate an environment—both externally and internally—that nurtures the best qualities in you.

✓ In this way, the "explosion" of good energy becomes the catalyst for your transformation, leading to a life where your actions, relationships, and very essence resonate with the divine light.

Child, remember that you are the gardener of your inner world. Choose carefully what you let in, for it will either nourish you or disrupt your balance. When you embrace positive exposure, the resulting explosion is not one of destruction but of creative, life-affirming transformation.

May you always seek out the rays of goodness, and may your inner light shine brightly, transforming every challenge into an opportunity for growth.

Chapter 69

KNOW YOU, KNOW ALL

The journey to self-awareness is the key that unlocks the mysteries of the universe. When we come to truly know ourselves— our strengths, weaknesses, desires, and fears—we also begin to understand the world around us. The deeper our understanding of our inner workings, the clearer our perception becomes of the world we live in. Every encounter, every challenge, and every joy is a mirror reflecting something within us. When we face ourselves honestly, we uncover the interconnectedness of all things.

To know yourself is to realize that you are not separate from the world, but part of a larger, divine whole. Your thoughts, actions, and energy ripple out into the universe, influencing the flow of life. In understanding yourself, you start to see the same patterns, behaviors, and truths mirrored in others. The world becomes less of a mystery when you recognize that what you see in others is often a reflection of what is within you.

When you know yourself deeply, you unlock the wisdom of the ages. You no longer feel lost in the chaos of life, for you understand that everything is interconnected. The more you explore your own mind and spirit, the more you realize that true knowledge and wisdom are not about external achievements, but about aligning with your authentic self. In this alignment, you see the world as it truly is, and in turn, you understand the meaning of life itself. Thus, to know yourself is to know all—because you are a part of the very fabric that weaves the universe together.

———•———

Swamy, you once said,

"When you cannot recognize yourself, you cannot recognize others; you only recognize yourself."

I understand that many who are self-absorbed or congested in their own ego fail to appreciate the talents and beauty in others— they boast of their abilities while ignoring the grace around them, much like a jasmine that never claims its own fragrance or beauty. Could you please explain what you truly mean by these words?

Swamy's Spirit Speaks

Child, this statement is a call to inner awareness and humility—a reminder that true vision begins with self-recognition and openness. Let me share the essence:

- **Self-Recognition as the Foundation**
  - If you do not know your own true nature, you are caught in the web of ego and illusion.
  - When you are overly preoccupied with your own self— your thoughts, desires, and limitations—you lose the ability to see the divine spark in others.
  - Self-recognition means understanding that your inner self is not separate from the universal truth. It is only when you see yourself clearly, with humility and insight, that you can truly appreciate the qualities of others.

◄ The Trap of Self-Absorption

- ✓ Many people, overwhelmed by their own concerns or inflated by their ego, end up only seeing themselves.

- ✓ This self-absorption blinds you to the unique talents, beauty, and grace that others possess.

- ✓ Just as a congested mind cannot perceive clarity, a heart full of self-interest cannot recognize the goodness in the world.

◄ The Example of the Jasmine

- ✓ Consider the jasmine flower, which quietly exudes its fragrance and beauty without boast or pretense.

- ✓ Its natural grace comes from being in tune with its essence, and it does not need to claim or compare itself with others.

- ✓ This is the ideal state of being—where you recognize that the beauty in others is a reflection of the divine that resides in all of us.

◄ The Deeper Message

- ✓ When you learn to recognize yourself—not in a narcissistic sense, but by understanding your true, interconnected nature—you open your heart to see the same divine essence in everyone else.

- ✓ This recognition dissolves the barriers of ego and leads to compassion, empathy, and genuine respect.

- ✓ In essence, true self-awareness is the gateway to universal vision. Once you see yourself clearly, you naturally see others as part of the same cosmic family, each with their own unique gifts.

Child, the journey is not about boasting or comparing; it is about awakening to your inner truth and, through that awakening, naturally recognizing and celebrating the divine spark in everyone. May you cultivate the humility to see beyond the self, and may your heart expand to embrace the beauty and talents of all beings.

Chapter 70

TIME SCRIPTS DESTINY

Time is the silent architect of our lives, shaping our past, present, and future with every moment that passes. It is within the flow of time that the seeds of our destiny are sown, watered, and nurtured. Every decision, every action, and every thought we have is a brushstroke on the canvas of our journey through time. While we may not always see the path clearly, time reveals it in its own divine rhythm—often when we least expect it.

Our destiny is not a singular moment but a continuous unfolding of experiences, woven together by the threads of time. In each phase of life, we are presented with opportunities to learn, grow, and transform. The key lies not in fighting against time, but in embracing it, understanding that each passing second contributes to the greater design of our life. The choices we make today ripple forward, influencing the destiny that lies ahead.

When we view time as a script, we realize that it is a guide, not a constraint. It is through the wise use of time that we craft a destiny aligned with our higher purpose. Just as a playwright carefully writes each act, time scripts our actions, and it is up to us to live with intention, mindfulness, and clarity. Time offers us a chance to shape our future—not by fighting against it, but by allowing it to guide us, trusting that each moment brings us closer to the fulfilment of our true potential.

Swamy, you said beautifully,

"Time is God, time is discipline, time is system, it is life and love, time is your future, time is silence, seek time to settle down, don't search to seek, but search to settle down."

I remember you mentioned this on the back of the photograph of Sri Sathya Sai when I met you at one of your disciples in Anantapur. Although I grasp its general essence, I would like to know its deeper meaning from your perspective—a truth that transcends ordinary comprehension. Please explain the inner message behind these words.

Swamy's Spirit Speaks

Child, these words are an invitation to see time not merely as a sequence of moments, but as a sacred, all-pervading force that shapes every aspect of our existence. Allow me to guide you through their deeper meaning:

- **Time is God**
  - ✓ Time is not just a measurement; it is the very expression of the Divine in motion.
  - ✓ Every moment holds the presence of the eternal, and by recognizing this, you begin to see that the divine is not separate from you—it flows through every second of your life.

◄ Time is Discipline

- ✓ Discipline is the art of harnessing time.
- ✓ When you honor and structure your time with mindfulness and commitment, you create the foundation for personal growth and spiritual evolution.
- ✓ It is through disciplined living that you learn to manage your energies and progress steadily on your path.

◄ Time is System

- ✓ The universe operates with a natural order—a cosmic system that governs the cycle of creation, dissolution, and renewal.
- ✓ Recognizing this system helps you understand that every event, every change, is part of a greater, orchestrated plan.
- ✓ This insight brings clarity and a sense of purpose to your daily activities.

◄ Time is Life and Love

- ✓ Life is made up of moments imbued with love, beauty, and the potential for transformation.
- ✓ By cherishing each moment as a gift, you infuse your life with the vitality of love, allowing your heart to bloom with gratitude and compassion.

◄ Time is Your Future

- ✓ Your actions in the present shape the future you will experience.
- ✓ Every decision, every effort, is a seed that grows over time, determining the quality of your life to come.

- ✓ This understanding encourages you to live consciously, aware that your choices have lasting impacts.

◄ **Time is Silence**

- ✓ In silence, the noise of the external world fades, and you are left with the still, profound presence of the Divine.

- ✓ It is in these quiet moments that the deepest truths are revealed, and you can connect with the eternal essence within you.

◄ **Seek Time to Settle Down:**

- ✓ Rather than being caught in the relentless rush of activity, you are invited to pause and find stillness.

- ✓ Settling down means aligning your inner state with the natural rhythm of the cosmos, allowing you to reflect, rejuvenate, and gain clarity.

◄ **Don't Search to Seek, But Search to Settle Down:**

- ✓ This means that the quest is not about chasing after time or external validations.

- ✓ Instead, focus on creating a space within yourself where peace and understanding naturally emerge.

- ✓ It is a call to embrace the present moment fully, letting go of the need to continually seek, and instead, to simply be.

Child, the beauty of these words is that they transform your perception of time from a mere ticking clock into a living, vibrant force that is intimately connected to your inner journey.

◄ When you see time as God, you realize that every moment is sacred.

- ◄ When you practice discipline with time, you empower yourself to grow steadily.

- ◄ When you align with the natural system of the universe, you discover the inherent order in life.

- ◄ When you embrace time as life and love, you open your heart to the fullness of existence.

- ◄ When you understand that time shapes your future, you are inspired to make conscious choices.

- ◄ And when you recognize the silence within time, you find the space to connect with the Divine.

May you always find the time to settle into the stillness of your soul, and may the sacred rhythm of the universe guide you to a life of profound peace, clarity, and everlasting love.

Chapter 71

BALANCE OF LIFE

The balance of life is the delicate harmony between all aspects of our existence—physical, mental, emotional, and spiritual. It is the understanding that life is not just about achieving success or acquiring material wealth, but about cultivating peace, purpose, and well-being in every moment. True balance comes when we integrate work, relationships, self-care, and spiritual growth, ensuring that none of these elements outweighs the others. Life is a constant ebb and flow, a dance of giving and receiving, and the balance of life encourages us to find peace in this flow, accepting both light and dark, joy and sorrow, as essential parts of the journey.

In our fast-paced world, where demands on time and energy often leave us feeling overwhelmed, the balance of life becomes even more crucial. It reminds us to slow down, reflect, and reconnect with what truly matters. When we live in balance, we are more mindful of our actions, more present in our relationships, and more attuned to our own inner needs. Balance is not about perfection, but about creating a space where all aspects of life are given attention and care. It involves learning to set boundaries, prioritize what is truly important, and allow ourselves the grace to rest, recharge, and restore our energy.

From a spiritual perspective, balance of life is about aligning ourselves with the natural rhythms of the universe. It is the realization that everything has its season—moments of action, moments of rest, moments of growth, and moments of retreat. Spiritual balance teaches us to surrender to the divine flow, trusting that everything happens for a reason, and that each experience has its purpose. By cultivating balance in our daily lives, we create space for divine wisdom to guide us, for love to flourish, and for peace to reside in our hearts. We learn to live not just for the moment, but in the moment, fully present and deeply connected to the divine presence in all things.

The balance of life is a journey, not a destination. It is a constant practice of being aware of ourselves, our surroundings, and the divine energy that flows through us. It teaches us that true fulfilment comes from living with intention and grace, nurturing all parts of our being, and finding joy in the simple act of being. When we embrace the balance of life, we create a life that is rich in meaning, harmony, and peace—a life that reflects the beauty of the universe itself.

Swamy, you often use sharp, transformative words with your devotees to awaken them, yet you also shower them with grace. I recall you once declared,

> **"Bake and become one, bring near, don't heat, benefit from your life, balance your mind, bring all near you, but be away from all, best is the balance of one's life, through body and words from your mouth."**

Is it possible to carry out this transformative process without the Guru's Grace? When we become instruments in the hands of

God, who truly does the work, and who ultimately receives the benefit?

Swamy's Spirit Speaks

Child, these words are a metaphor for the inner alchemy required to transform your being. They describe a process of purifying and aligning your life that, while challenging, is the very path to union with the Divine. Let me explain each part:

- **"Bake and become one"**
  - ✓ Think of "baking" as a process of refinement—just as raw dough transforms into nourishing bread under heat, your inner self must undergo the transformative fire of experience.
  - ✓ This "baking" melts away the rigid layers of ego and ignorance, allowing you to merge with the universal truth and become one with the Divine.

- **"Bring near, don't heat"**
  - ✓ To "bring near" means to invite the Divine presence into your heart through sincere practices like devotion, meditation, and selfless service.
  - ✓ "Don't heat" cautions you against letting passion or uncontrolled emotions disturb the balance you need to maintain.
  - ✓ It is a call to welcome divine energy gently without getting carried away by the storms of the mind.

- **"Benefit from your life"**
  - ✓ Every moment, whether joyful or challenging, carries the seed of a lesson from the Divine.

- ✓ By learning from these experiences, you transform them into opportunities for inner growth and wisdom.

◁ **"Balance your mind"**

- ✓ A balanced mind is like a calm lake that reflects the sky.
- ✓ When you maintain mental equilibrium, you can perceive reality clearly and respond to life with measured compassionate action.

◁ **"Bring all near you, but be away from all"**

- ✓ This paradox encourages you to recognize the oneness of all creation—seeing the Divine in every being—while also practising detachment.
- ✓ You are to engage with the world without being ensnared by its transient attachments, remaining free and unaffected by external fluctuations.

◁ **"Best is the balance of one's life, through body and words from your mouth"**

- ✓ True transformation is reflected in every aspect of your being—your actions, your speech, and your very presence.
- ✓ When your life is balanced, you express a natural harmony that uplifts both yourself and those around you.

Now, you ask whether this process can be accomplished without the Guru's Grace. Child, the journey of inner transformation is subtle and intricate; the Guru's Grace acts as the illuminating light that reveals and supports this process.

≺ Without such grace, the path becomes arduous, for the inner work of dissolving the ego and cultivating balance is not easily navigated on your own.

≺ **When you become an instrument in the hands of God, it is the Divine that ultimately does the work.**

  ✓ Your role is to be receptive, to engage wholeheartedly in the process of self-purification and to allow your inner light to shine.

≺ **Who receives the benefit?**

  ✓ You, the sincere seeker, are the one who absorbs the transformative energy.

  ✓ The benefits—peace, wisdom, and unity—flow into your being as you align with the Divine will.

Child, while you initiate the journey with your own effort, it is through the Guru's Grace—and ultimately, the grace of God—that the full transformation occurs. May you always remain open to divine guidance, trusting that as you refine your inner self, the universal energy will work through you to create a life of balance, oneness, and profound fulfilment.

Chapter 72

TRUE CHARACTER

True character is not shaped in moments of ease but revealed in times of challenge. It is not built by mere words but by the quiet strength of our actions, especially when no one is watching. The world may admire talent, intelligence, and success, but it is integrity, kindness, and unwavering courage that truly define a person. Appearances may deceive, but life has a way of testing the unseen—the honesty in small choices, the resilience in setbacks, and the humility in triumph.

Character is not about seeking approval or pleasing the world; it is about standing firm in truth, even when it is difficult. Like a mighty tree that bends in the storm but never breaks, a person of true character remains unshaken by praise or criticism. It is not about perfection, but about choosing what is right over what is easy, compassion over selfishness, and purpose over comfort. In the end, everything fades— power, wealth, and status—but character endures. It is the only wealth time cannot steal, the only legacy that truly matters.

Swamy, you often tell your spiritual aspirants,

"The depth of your character is revealed in the way you respond to situations you dislike."

What is the deeper meaning behind this? Can you reveal its inner essence?

Swamy's Spirit Speaks

Character is not tested in moments of ease but in the fire of discomfort. **It is not how you act when everything goes your way that defines you, but how you respond when things do not.**

Life does not move according to your desires alone. Situations arise that challenge your patience, provoke your emotions, and test your stability. **A shallow mind reacts; a deep mind responds.** Reaction is instinctive, driven by impulses, but response is cultivated—it comes from awareness and mastery of the self.

If you dislike a situation, pause. Observe your thoughts. Does anger arise? Does frustration cloud your mind? These emotions are not the problem; your identification with them is. When a storm rages in the sky, the vast ocean remains undisturbed in its depths. **The depth of your character is determined by how steady you remain when the winds of life blow against you.**

To respond with grace is to elevate the self beyond the moment. It is to see discomfort not as an enemy but as a teacher, revealing your strengths and weaknesses. Those who react are bound by circumstance; those who respond wisely are free.

True spiritual maturity is when your inner peace is untouched by outer chaos. When you cultivate this, no situation—pleasant or unpleasant—can disturb the stillness of your being. This is strength, this is wisdom, and this is the essence of true character.

Chapter 73

KEEP THE DREAM ALIVE

Dreams are the light that guide us, the hope that keeps us moving forward. They are not meant to be abandoned when challenges arise or traded for an easier path. The journey toward any dream will have struggles—failures, doubts, and moments of uncertainty. But dreams only fade when we stop believing in them.

Keeping a dream alive means trusting in it, even when the road gets tough. It means learning from mistakes, rising after every fall, and moving forward step by step. Success does not happen overnight, and obstacles are just part of the journey. Those who keep going, despite the difficulties, are the ones who turn dreams into reality.

No dream is too big, and no effort is wasted. Hold on, believe in yourself, and keep moving. The world belongs to those who never give up.

Swamy, you often say with a smile,

"The highest temptation in life is to convert dreams into reality, but the greatest flaw in life's journey is when we surrender our dreams to reality."

This statement sounds profound yet complex. Can you simplify it so that I can truly understand its essence?

Swamy's Spirit Speaks

Child, this teaching is about preserving the purity and inspiration of your dreams while remaining flexible enough to grow. Let me break it down simply:

- **The Highest Temptation – Converting Dreams into Reality**
  - ✓ Often, you are tempted to grab hold of your dreams and force them to materialize exactly as you imagined.
  - ✓ This desire to turn dreams into something concrete can be alluring because it promises the fulfilment of our deepest aspirations.
  - ✓ However, when you try too hard to make your dream fit into the confines of what you already know, you risk losing its creative, inspiring quality.
- **The Greatest Flaw – Surrendering Your Dreams to Reality**
  - ✓ On the other hand, if you let your dreams become completely absorbed by the limitations and compromises of everyday reality, they lose their spark.
  - ✓ Surrendering your dreams to reality means allowing external circumstances—such as fear, doubt, or societal expectations—to dictate what your dreams should be.

- ✓ When that happens, the original vision, the vibrant possibility of what could be, fades away into something ordinary.

- ◁ **The Balance to Seek**
  - ✓ The ideal is to **let your dreams inspire you** while staying open and adaptable to life's flow.

  - ✓ Use your dreams as a guiding star—something that fuels your inner growth and creativity—without becoming so rigidly attached that they lose their magic.

  - ✓ Think of it as holding a beautiful, delicate flower: you admire its beauty and let it uplift your spirit, but you do not try to force it to bloom in a way that stifles its natural grace.

- ◁ **In Practical Terms**
  - ✓ **Nurture Your Vision:** Keep your dreams alive by allowing them to evolve with you.

  - ✓ **Stay Flexible:** Be open to change and growth; let your aspirations guide you, not bind you.

  - ✓ **Balance Action and Imagination:** Work steadily towards your goals, but don't let the pressure of making everything "real" diminish the wonder and possibility in your heart.

Child, the true essence of my words is to remind you that while dreams are powerful and can light the path to a fulfilled life, they must be handled with care. Preserve the imaginative, boundless quality of your dreams, yet be willing to let them transform naturally as you journey through life. This balance between aspiration and flexibility is where true growth and fulfilment reside.

May you always nurture your dreams without losing their magic, and may you walk your path with both determination and an open, creative heart.

Chapter 74

DEATH IS TRANSFORMATION

*D*eath is often feared, misunderstood, and shrouded in mystery, but from a spiritual perspective, it is not an end but a profound transformation. Just as the seasons cycle through birth, growth, decay, and renewal, so too does life move through phases of existence. Death marks a transition, not an expiration. It is a powerful shift in energy, a redefinition of form, but not the end of being.

In the physical world, death may appear as the cessation of life, the breaking of the body's systems, but in the spiritual realm, death is seen as a gateway to higher consciousness and a return to the source. It is the shedding of an old self to make room for a new phase of existence. The soul, according to many spiritual traditions, does not perish with the body but continues on its journey, evolving and growing through each experience.

Death is transformation because it frees us from the limitations of our physical form. Just like a butterfly that must leave behind its cocoon to soar, our soul must release its earthly shell to experience the vastness of the universe. In this sense, death is not a loss, but a movement toward a higher state of being, a return to the divine source from which we came. It is a transition to unity, peace, and an eternal state of consciousness, where time, space, and separation cease to exist.

On a practical level, understanding death as transformation invites us to live more fully. It teaches us that life is not about clinging to the temporary, but about embracing the transient nature of all things. This awareness encourages us to let go of attachments, to live with purpose and love, and to seek the deeper meaning beyond the material world. We come to realize that death is not something to fear, but something to accept with grace, as part of the natural order and as a reminder of the impermanence of all things.

In the end, death is not the end of the soul's journey but a necessary step toward spiritual evolution and enlightenment. Through death, we transcend the illusion of separateness and re-enter the boundless oneness of existence. The energy we put into life—our thoughts, actions, and love—transforms into a higher vibrational force that continues to shape the universe long after our physical departure. Embracing death as transformation reminds us that life, in all its forms, is a sacred journey, leading us to the ultimate realization of truth, peace, and unity.

Swamy, you once said,

"Change of body is called death."

I understand that this event comes knocking on one's door whether one is interested or not. Even my brother, Naga Yogi Raj—a saint with hidden radiance—has said that his soul is so strong it does not remain confined within the body. I have doubts about what you mean by this. Could you please explain and clarify the deeper meaning behind this statement?

Swamy's Spirit Speaks

Child, the statement **"Change of body is called death"** is a profound reminder of the transient nature of our physical form and the eternal journey of the soul. Let me explain its inner essence:

- **The Transience of the Body**
  - ✓ Your body is like a temporary vessel, a garment that you wear for a season.
  - ✓ When that garment no longer serves its purpose, it is shed, and a new one is donned.
  - ✓ This shedding of the body is what we call death—not an end, but a natural transition from one form to another.

- **The Eternal Soul**
  - ✓ The soul is the unchanging, divine essence that resides within you.
  - ✓ It is not limited by the physical form; it is vast, enduring, and capable of transcending the material world.
  - ✓ When I say, "change of body is called death," I remind you that the true self—the soul—continues its journey beyond the temporary confines of the body.

- **Naga Yogi Raj's Insight**
  - ✓ As your brother, Naga Yogi Raj, has expressed, his soul is so strong that it is not meant to be confined within one physical form.
  - ✓ This insight reflects the timeless truth that the soul's power and essence far exceed the limitations of the body.

✓ It is a call to recognize that while the body may change or cease to function, the soul remains eternal and continues its evolution in different forms and experiences.

◁ Understanding Death as Transformation

✓ Death, therefore, is not a terminal end but a transformation—a necessary step in the cyclical journey of life.

✓ It is an opportunity for the soul to shed the old, learn from its experiences, and prepare for new beginnings.

✓ This perspective encourages you to focus on the growth and evolution of your inner self rather than fear the inevitable changes in your physical form.

◁ The Deeper Message for Your Journey

✓ By understanding that the body is transient and the soul eternal, you can cultivate a deeper sense of detachment and inner peace.

✓ This knowledge invites you to invest in your spiritual growth, knowing that the challenges of the physical realm are temporary, while the journey of the soul is everlasting.

✓ It also reassures you that every change, every end, is simply part of a larger, divine plan—one that is ultimately aimed at your liberation and evolution.

Child, do not fear the change of the body. Instead, embrace it as a natural, sacred process that allows your eternal soul to continue its magnificent journey.

May this understanding bring you comfort and inspire you to focus on the inner light that is your true self, ever unbound by the limitations of the material world.

Chapter 75

THE RIPPLE EFFECT OF ACTIONS

Every action we take, no matter how small, sends out ripples into the world, affecting people, situations, and even the course of events in ways we may never fully understand. Like a stone thrown into a calm lake, our choices can stir far-reaching waves of impact. A simple smile, a kind word, or an act of generosity may seem insignificant in the moment, but its effects often extend far beyond what we see.

In life, our actions have the power to shape the world around us. Just as a ripple grows larger as it moves outward, our intentions—whether positive or negative—create a chain reaction that can touch many lives. A single moment of compassion can inspire others to act with kindness, and a decision made with integrity can influence others to pursue righteousness. Each action is a thread in the fabric of human experience, weaving connections that bind us all together in this journey of life.

Spiritually, the ripple effect teaches us the profound truth that we are all interconnected. Every action we take, every thought we nurture, contributes to the collective energy of the universe. By living with awareness and intentionality, we have the power to cultivate positive change and spread peace, love, and wisdom throughout the world. Our actions may seem small, but their impact is immeasurable, reminding us that we are all part of a larger, interconnected whole.

Swamy, you once said,

"Society is accountable at all levels—this accountability is evident in our day-to-day activities, among kings, rulers, political leaders, and the media."

I understand that by society you mean all people, but you mentioned kings, and I wonder: where are these kings now? I find it difficult to fully appreciate or understand your message. Please, with your love, clarify my doubts.

Swamy's Spirit Speaks

Child, my words point to a timeless principle—that every part of society, from the smallest interaction to the highest authority, is bound by the law of accountability. Let me explain:

◁ **Accountability in Society**

- ✓ When I speak of society being accountable, I refer to the idea that every action, whether by an individual or a collective, contributes to the unfolding of a greater order.

- ✓ In ancient times, kings and rulers embodied the highest authority and were held responsible for the welfare of their people. Although the form of leadership has evolved over time, the fundamental principle remains: those in positions of power must answer for their actions.

✓ Today, while we may no longer see literal kings on thrones, the spirit of leadership endures in our political leaders, corporate heads, and community influencers. Their decisions, like those of the kings of old, affect the fabric of society.

◄ The Role of the Media

✓ The media, as I mentioned, is also accountable. It serves as a bridge between those in power and the people, reflecting and scrutinizing actions and decisions.

✓ Accountability here means that information should be transparent and that power should not go unchecked. The media is one of the vital channels through which society maintains its balance and integrity.

◄ The Deeper Message

✓ The mention of kings is symbolic—it represents authority and responsibility. Even if the titles have changed, the concept remains: every leader, every institution, every individual has a duty to act rightly and justly.

✓ In our modern world, this accountability is embedded in our legal systems, our ethical standards, and the collective conscience of society.

✓ The essence of my message is that no matter the form, every segment of society is interwoven with responsibility. The actions of those in power—be they ancient kings or contemporary leaders—shape the destiny of all.

✓ Moreover, you must understand that accountability is not solely imposed from without; it is a call for each of you to hold yourselves to a higher standard to act with integrity and awareness in every aspect of life.

Child, do not be disheartened by the shifting forms of authority. The eternal truth remains that every action has consequences, and the collective welfare depends on the integrity of every individual. Whether it is a king of old or a modern leader, accountability is the backbone of a just and harmonious society.

May you always strive to act with wisdom and integrity, knowing that true leadership is not measured by titles but by the quality of your actions and your commitment to the greater good.

Chapter 76

FROM WORDS TO WISDOM: SEEKING THE TRUE PATH IN SPIRITUALITY

Spirituality is not about eloquent words or external rituals but about inner transformation. Many speak of Vedanta, but few embody its essence. True wisdom is not in preaching but in living the truth. His Holiness Sri Vidyanarayana Theertha reminds us that mere  *intellectual discussions on Vedanta are of little value if they do not lead to self-awareness and genuine change. A seeker must not stop at learning concepts but must strive to experience and integrate them into daily life.*

The journey toward wisdom begins with the right approach to learning. A Guru imparts knowledge, a Sadguru awakens realization, and a Gurudev embodies the divine truth. While many are drawn to spiritual figures, the real question is: Do we seek the body or the soul? Do we admire the external presence of a Guru, or do we absorb the wisdom he imparts? True discipleship is not about proximity to the Guru but about internalizing his teachings with sincerity and authenticity.

1. **Truth is a Journey, Not a Destination**

   "The path to truth is not found in a single book, teacher, or belief. It unfolds through experience, reflection, and sincere seeking."

2. **Silence Holds More Than Words**

   "In silence, the soul speaks. The more we quiet the mind, the clearer the truth becomes."

3. **Faith and Doubt Are Companions**

   "True seekers do not fear doubt; they embrace it as a stepping stone to deeper understanding."

4. **Wisdom is Lived, Not Just Learned**

   "Spiritual knowledge means nothing if it does not transform your heart and actions."

5. **Light Comes from Within**

   "The answers you seek are not outside of you—they are waiting within, in the depths of your own being."

6. **Let Go to Grow**

   "Clinging to old beliefs out of fear blocks new insights. True wisdom requires the courage to unlearn and grow."

7. **Love is the Highest Truth**

   "No spiritual path is true if it does not lead to love, compassion, and kindness toward all beings."

Seeking the Essence of Swamiji's Words: A Reflection

Swamy, I humbly asked you, **"Why do you continue to give these messages? They are my food for the soul."** In response, you shared the profound message you had given to your disciples at Tirupati:

"People don't teach, but they preach Vedanta.

Why are people after Swamiji?

Is it because of the body or the soul?

I think it is the body.

Let us act openly.

Let us not pretend to act."

Swamiji's words invite deep contemplation. What does he truly mean? What insight does he wish to impart to his disciples? Is he questioning the sincerity of seekers, urging them to reflect on whether they are drawn to the external presence of a Guru or to the wisdom he embodies? Is he reminding us that spirituality is not about appearances but about genuine transformation?

What lesson does he want his disciples to internalize? Is he cautioning against superficial devotion, where people revere a Guru outwardly but fail to embrace his teachings in their hearts? Is he calling for authenticity in spiritual practice—where one does not merely act pious but truly lives the wisdom of Vedanta?

Swamiji, your words stir my soul. I pray to you—guide me to see beyond the illusion of form, to seek truth beyond appearances, and to walk the path of sincere learning and self-realization.

The Spirit of Swamy answers

1. **The Contrast Between Teaching and Preaching**

   "People don't teach, but they preach Vedanta."

   Swamiji highlights the fundamental difference between true teaching and mere preaching. Teaching involves transmitting knowledge through lived experience, guiding others by example, and enabling them to discover truth within. Preaching, on the other hand, is often limited to words and intellectual discussion without personal transformation.

Example: A teacher who genuinely embodies Vedanta will inspire change simply through their presence, like Adi Shankaracharya, who didn't just expound Advaita but lived it completely. In contrast, many today speak eloquently about Vedanta but fail to integrate its essence into their daily lives.

Lesson: True seekers must strive to internalize Vedantic principles rather than discuss them. Spirituality must be a lived experience, not a mere topic of debate.

2. **The Guru, the Sadguru, and the Gurudev – Understanding Their Roles**

Not all guides are the same in spiritual life. Swamiji's message makes us question who we follow and why.

◈ **Guru** – A teacher who imparts knowledge and guides seekers in their spiritual journey. A guru provides light in the initial stages, much like a lamp in darkness.

◈ **Sadguru** – A realized master who not only teaches but awakens the disciple's inner wisdom. A Sadguru doesn't just give knowledge but leads the seeker toward direct experience of the truth.

◈ **Gurudev** – A divine master whose presence alone can transform lives. A Gurudev doesn't merely teach or guide— he *is* the embodiment of the highest truth. His grace transcends intellect, pulling the seeker beyond mind and ego.

Example: In Swami Vivekananda's life, his guru was Sri Ramakrishna, who guided him in Vedanta. But Ramakrishna was not just a guru; he was a *Sadguru* who ignited direct realization in Vivekananda. For his disciples, he was also *Gurudev*—one who embodied the divine itself.

Lesson: Seekers must differentiate between learning from a teacher (*guru*), experiencing wisdom through a realized master (*Sadguru*), and surrendering to a divine force (*Gurudev*). One must not stop at mere intellectual learning but strive for true transformation.

3. **The Question of Devotion: Body vs. Soul**

"Why are people after Swamiji? Is it because of the body or the soul? I think it is the body."

Swamiji poses a deep question that every disciple must reflect upon: Why do we seek a Guru? Is it for his physical presence, his status, or the comfort of being associated with a spiritual figure? Or do we genuinely seek the wisdom and transformation that his teachings offer?

Example: Many flock to spiritual leaders, seeking blessings for worldly gains—health, wealth, success—but few truly seek liberation (*moksha*). Just as people crowded around Sri Ramakrishna Paramahamsa, some sought miracles, while only a few, like Swami Vivekananda, absorbed his wisdom and became torchbearers of his teachings.

Lesson: True discipleship lies in seeking the soul's wisdom, not just being physically close to the Guru. Real devotion is about embodying the Guru's teachings, not idolizing his external form.

4. A Call for Authenticity and Transparency

"Let us act openly. Let us not pretend to act."

Swamiji calls for sincerity in spiritual life. Many pretend to be spiritual—chanting mantras, attending satsangs, or adopting religious attire—without true inner transformation. He warns against this superficiality, urging seekers to act with honesty and integrity.

> **Example:** A person may sit for meditation but remain restless, thinking of worldly matters. Another may recite scriptures but fail to practice compassion. Just as a fruit's fragrance reveals its ripeness, true spirituality is revealed in one's conduct, not appearances.

> **Lesson:** Spiritual growth requires honesty. One must genuinely strive for self-realization instead of pretending to be evolved. True seekers should be courageous in self-examination and remove layers of hypocrisy.

Final Reflection – The Path to True Spirituality

Swamiji's message is a wake-up call for every seeker. He urges us to:

- **Live Vedanta, not just speak of it.**
- **Seek the eternal soul, not the temporary body.**
- **Be authentic in spiritual practice, not performative.**

A Prayer to Swamiji:

O Beloved Swamiji

O Beloved Swamiji,

You, who see beyond illusion,

Guide us to seek the soul, not the shell,

To embrace wisdom, not just to tell.

May we learn, not merely preach,

Walk the path, not just teach.

With hearts sincere, with vision bright,

May we act in truth, not hide in sight.

Awaken us to Vedanta's light,

Beyond the shadows, beyond the night.

Let pretense fade, let wisdom shine,

In your grace, we walk divine.

Chapter 77

KARMA, DHARMA, AND DIVINE PLAY

Life presents us with challenges, uncertainties, and moments of suffering, often leaving us questioning the divine play behind them. Why does God sometimes lead devotees through difficult paths? How does karma shape our experiences? What is the essence of Sanatana Dharma in navigating good and evil?

Through the profound words of His Holiness Sri Vidyanarayana Theertha, we seek to uncover the deeper truths hidden in these questions. Rooted in the principles of karma, dharma, and Divine Leela, Swamy's discourse offers insights into the unseen forces at work in our lives. By understanding the connection between spiritual wisdom and even scientific principles, we gain clarity on our journey.

This discourse serves as a guide to embracing faith, recognizing the role of karma, and understanding how righteousness (dharma) should be upheld in all aspects of life. Swamy's spirit speaks—answering with wisdom, revealing the unseen, and guiding seekers toward self-awareness and divine realization.

Swamy's Spirit Answers

1. **Why does God sometimes lead devotees through difficult and critical situations?**

◈ *We often ask, "Why me?" when facing hardships. Why does God, whom we seek for protection, allow suffering?*

Swamy's Spirit Answers

Have you ever seen a potter shaping a clay pot? He presses and beats the clay, but it is not out of cruelty. It is to give it strength. Similarly, God allows us to go through trials to mould us into something greater.

Example:

Prahlada, a young child, faced immense suffering from his father, Hiranyakashipu. But what happened in the end? His faith remained unshaken, and God himself appeared as Narasimha to protect him. What looked like suffering was actually a test of devotion.

So, instead of asking, "Why is this happening to me?" ask, "What is God teaching me through this?"

2. **How does the karma theory relate to suffering?**

People often say, "This is my fate," but is karma a punishment? If every action has a reaction, how does this affect our lives?

Swamy's Spirit Answers

Karma is not about punishment or reward but a law of balance. If you throw a ball against a wall, what happens? It comes back with the same force. Similarly, every thought, word, and deed has consequences, though we may not see them immediately.

Example:

King Dasharatha once accidentally killed a young boy while hunting. The boy's blind parents cursed him that he too would suffer the loss of his son. Many years later, this unfolded when Lord Rama was sent into exile.

But here's the deeper truth: Karma is not to make us suffer but to help us learn. A wise person sees karma as an opportunity to grow.

3. What is the purpose of suffering? Is it to learn, gain experience, or see the bigger picture?

◆ *When we suffer, we only see the pain. But could there be a larger purpose?*

Swamy's Spirit Answers

Let's say a mother takes her child for a vaccination. The child cries, thinking, "Why is my mother allowing this pain?" But the mother knows it is for the child's well-being. Similarly, suffering often prepares us for something greater.

Example:

Kunti Devi, the mother of the Pandavas, prayed to Krishna: *"Give me difficulties, for in difficulties, I remember you the most."* She understood that suffering brings us closer to truth.

Next time you face hardships, instead of resisting, ask, *"What lesson is hidden in this?"*

4. How does God's divine play (Leela) relate to physics—especially action and reaction?

Can spiritual truths be explained scientifically? How does Leela relate to physics?

Swamy's Spirit Answers

The universe is built on laws, both seen and unseen. Newton's law states: *For every action, there is an equal and opposite reaction.* The same applies to karma.

Example:

Ravana abducted Sita, believing he was powerful. But what happened? The same force he used against Dharma led to his downfall. His own actions brought about his end.

Even in daily life, if we act with anger, we receive anger in return. If we act with love, love returns. This is how God's play (Leela) is woven into the laws of nature.

5. Why do we struggle to understand the consequences of karma while experiencing its effects?

If karma is so simple, why don't we understand it when we are suffering?

Swamy's Spirit Answers

Imagine walking into a movie halfway through. You see a character suffering but don't know what happened earlier. Similarly, when we experience karma, we don't see the full story—we only see the present pain.

Example:

A farmer plants a seed and expects a harvest. But does he see the result immediately? No. Similarly, karma is a cycle. Just because we don't see its origin doesn't mean it doesn't exist.

Instead of questioning, "Why is this happening now?" try asking, *"What do I need to learn from this moment?"*

6. **Who are the Rakshasas (demons) and Devatas (divine beings) in today's world?**

   Are Rakshasas and Devatas only mythological, or do they exist around us today?

Swamy's Spirit Answers

Rakshasas are not just beings from ancient stories. They exist in human form—as greed, selfishness, and cruelty. Devatas, on the other hand, exist as kindness, selflessness, and wisdom.

Example:

A corrupt leader who exploits people for personal gain is a Rakshasa. A teacher who selflessly educates poor children is a Devata.

So, the real question is: *Which one are we feeding within ourselves—the Rakshasa or the Devata?*

7. **How should one follow Sanatana Dharma properly?**

   Does following Sanatana Dharma mean just performing rituals? Or is there something deeper?

Swamy's Spirit Answers

True Dharma is not in external rituals but in internal transformation. Worship is not just lighting lamps—it is lighting the lamp of wisdom within.

Example:

A person may visit temples daily but still lie and cheat. Another may never visit a temple but live truthfully and selflessly. Who is truly following Dharma?

Rituals are tools, but the essence of Dharma is in living with righteousness.

8. What does 'awareness' mean in our Shastras, and how should it be shared?

We talk about spreading awareness, but what does it really mean?

Swamy's Spirit Answers

Awareness is not just intellectual knowledge—it is realization. It is seeing things as they truly are, beyond illusion.

Example:

Adi Shankaracharya did not just debate about scriptures—he awakened people to the truth within themselves.

To spread awareness, we must live it first. A candle that is not lit cannot light another.

9. Why is the Bhagavad Gita difficult to understand? How can one develop true faith and trust in it?

Many read the Gita, but few understand it. Why?

Swamy's Spirit Answers

The Gita is not just a book—it is a mirror. Understanding it requires an open heart, not just an intellectual mind.

Example:

Arjuna, despite being a great warrior, was confused and fearful. Only when he surrendered and said, *"Krishna, I trust you,"* did wisdom dawn upon him.

Similarly, if we approach the Gita with love and trust, its teachings will reveal themselves naturally.

Mangalam to the Divine Guide

Mangalam Vasudevaya, *the light so pure,*

The one who heals, the hearts obscure.

In every step, in joy or strife,

He leads us through the dance of life.

Mangalam Nandasunave, *the child so bright,*

Born to bless, to spread His light.

Through love and grace, He walks our way,

A guiding star that never sways.

Mangalam Parthasuthaya, *the charioteer wise,*

Who clears the veil from blinded eyes.

In war, in doubt, His voice is near,

Dispelling darkness, conquering fear.

Geetacharyaya Mangalam, *the song divine,*

Echoing truth through endless time.

To love, to trust, to care and see,

The Gita's path shall set us free.

May we not just seek knowledge but truly experience wisdom. May Swamy's words guide us to truth, clarity, and peace.

FROM SELF TO SELFLESS: THE DIVINE JOURNEY OF HIS HOLINESS SRI VIDYANARAYANA THEERTHA SWAMY

A STORY OF A SOUL THAT DID NOT SEEK TO RISE ABOVE OTHERS, BUT TO SINK INTO THE SOURCE WITHIN.

INTRODUCTION: A JOURNEY ROOTED IN SILENCE, BLOSSOMING INTO SERVICE

In a world obsessed with achievement, His Holiness Sri Vidyanarayana Theertha Swamy stands as a radiant exception. A doctor by profession, a mystic by destiny, and a sanyasi by surrender—his life is not a linear tale of success, but a circular unfolding of inner truth. He didn't walk away from the world in renunciation; he walked deeper into its pain, its illusions, and its possibilities—armed not with ambition, but with awareness.

He performed yagnas, homas, and intense tapasya—not to gain merit or public acclaim, but to cleanse karmic fields, rebalance elemental disharmony, and uplift the collective human spirit. His journey is not a retreat from reality, but a return to what is real.

"I did not seek to become a sanyasi. I simply allowed myself to embrace the truth that was always within me, letting go of the illusion of separation and ego."

A Lifetime of Service: Fifty Years of Sacred Commitment

Our Pujya Sri Swamiji, Sri Sri Sri Vidyanarayana Theertha, has dedicated the last 50 years to the path of spiritual upliftment in a truly divine and transformative way. Realizing the eternal truth, he embraced renunciation and became a *Sanathana Yatheeswara*, a monk rooted in the timeless traditions of Indian spirituality. With unwavering discipline and devotion, he has completed **50 Chaturmasya Vrathas**, exemplifying steadfast commitment to the spiritual path.

From a humble beginning in a remote village, Swamiji established an educational institution that runs from 1st to 12th standard—offering not just academic instruction, but a curriculum embedded with the eternal values of *Sanathana Dharma*. In his school, children are taught not only to read and write but to **respect parents and teachers**, to **live aligned with Dharma and Karma**, and to **honor the spiritual essence of our Hindu traditions**.

The Journey Unfolds: From Healing the Body to Healing the World

Swamy began his life in the structured world of modern medicine, guided by clinical reasoning and diagnostics. Yet, beyond the symptoms of disease, he began to witness deeper wounds—those of the soul. This realization marked a turning point: he transitioned from being a physician who treats, to a seer who transforms.

Let us walk through the essence of his journey across key spiritual dimensions:

1. **True Renunciation: Beyond the Robes**

   Swamy's renunciation wasn't an event. It was an evaporation. He didn't drop the world; the illusion of separation dropped from him. As identity dissolved, compassion arose.

   "Renunciation begins when you stop asking, 'What do I get?' and start living, 'What can I give?'"

2. **Yagnas, Homas, and Tapasya: Not for Display but for Dharma**

   He performed sacred rituals not as rituals, but as rhythmic responses to cosmic imbalance. Homas for healing waters. Yagnas for inner light. Tapasya for invoking alignment in a misaligned age.

   "Let every fire I light burn not my ego, but the veils that blind others."

   His austerities were not personal *sadhana* alone—they were offerings to humanity.

3. **Sanatana Dharma: Not in Labels but in Living**

   Swamy lives *Sanatana Dharma* as a living consciousness—not a doctrine, caste, or inherited pride. For him, *dharma* is the daily practice of truth, humility, and compassion. Not inherited by birth—but awakened by inner fire.

   "Dharma is not what you are born into. It's what you are brave enough to live by."

Sanathana Dharma, as Swamiji teaches, is the **eternal code of righteous living**, rooted in one's nature and duty. Whether a washerman, farmer, barber, Kshatriya, Vaishya, or Brahmin, every role is sacred when performed with sincerity.

Dharma does not divide; it **unites**.

4. **Karma: Work is Worship**

Karma is action performed in alignment with Dharma. Swamiji often says:

"Do your Karma. God will bless you."

God has given each of us a divine duty. A farmer must farm. A teacher must teach. A doctor must heal. Each profession is sacred. Not interfering in another's duty, but respecting and doing one's own work with sincerity—is true Karma Yoga.

Karma is not just work—it is worship.

5. **The Four Ashramas: A Complete Life Model**

Swamiji has consistently taught and demonstrated the value of the *fourfold path of life*, known as **Ashrama Dharma**:

1. **Brahmachari** – Learn, practice discipline, and build values.

2. **Gruhastha** – Fulfill duties to family and society with Dharma.

3. **Vanaprastha** – Gradually detach and guide the younger generation.

4. **Sanyasi** – Renounce material ties and dedicate oneself to spiritual awakening.

Swamiji has guided countless individuals through these transitions, proving by example that a complete human life is one of **balance, humility, and divine purpose**.

6. **Equality: The Soul Knows No Caste**

   With piercing clarity, Swamy shatters hierarchical illusions:

   "No one is high. No one is low. Only your awareness has heights."

   He rejects any framework that places one human above another based on birth, role, or ritual knowledge. Spirituality begins where ego ends.

7. **The Feminine Principle: Reverence, Not Ritual**

   To Swamy, the Divine Mother is not a festival icon but the **pulse of Dharma**.

   He urges us to **restore the place of women**—not just in temples, but in our daily decisions and institutions.

   "Do not ask where the goddess lives—ask whether she is welcome in your decisions."

8. **Patience and Silence: Anchors of Inner Evolution**

   Swamy's spiritual force lies not in loud sermons, but in quiet presence. In a time of rush and display, his silence speaks more.

   "Be still enough, and truth will no longer whisper—it will thunder within you."

9. **Truth as Action, Not Argument**

   Swamy does not argue philosophy. He lives it.

   "If your truth needs defending, it's not yet deep enough. When you live it, it shines on its own."

   His life is a scripture written not in ink, but in action.

Key Insights: The Mystic Thread Unveiled

⊲ **Ritual with Purpose**

Homas and yagnas as energy medicine—not ceremony.

- **Renunciation by Realization**

  Walking away isn't renunciation—*waking up* is.

- **Dharma is a Lived Truth**

  It's not a costume—it's daily character.

- **Woman = Shakti = Dharma's Pulse**

  Dharma cannot stand where the feminine is ignored.

- **All Souls Are Equal**

  Birth is accidental. Awareness is intentional.

- **Silence Speaks Loudest**

  Loudness proves ego. Silence reveals the soul.

- **Spirituality is Not a Show**

  If you're explaining too much, you're not embodying enough.

- **Transformation is for Service**

  His moksha is not his own—but a light for all.

A Global Call for Peace and Harmony

Swamiji often speaks of the unrest both inside and outside the world, urging that the time has come for each of us to contribute to a global society where peace, safety, justice, and harmony prevail. We must look inward and ask: *What can I give, rather than what can I take?* It is the joy of sharing, caring, and being aware of our collective responsibility to society that will create the change we seek. We often suggest others should change, but fail to change ourselves. The more we awaken to this truth, the more the world becomes ours, and together we make a bigger difference.

Conclusion: A Call for Change and Service

The life of His Holiness Sri Vidyanarayana Theertha Swamy is more than just an inspiring story; it is a living message for all of us. He did not leave the world; he embraced it in its purest form, aligning himself with deeper truths. From being a doctor to a sanyasi, Swamiji showed us that true greatness is not found in material success, but in surrendering the ego and serving the greater good.

His teachings, preserved in four profound books, continue to guide us, not as words on paper, but as living principles that we can apply every day. Swamiji's life is a perfect example of how to live with purpose, compassion, and humility. His actions speak louder than any words could.

Swamiji often says:

"True happiness comes not from what we accumulate, but from how we live in alignment with higher truth. Teach your children Dharma, but also live it in every moment. This is the way to true peace."

In these times of uncertainty and global unrest, the path Swamiji showed us holds more importance than ever. The world is calling out for peace, harmony, and justice. The time has come for each of us to take responsibility—not just for our own lives, but for the world we share. By embracing simplicity, service, and truth, we can create a world where safety is ensured, equality prevails, and compassion reigns.

Swamiji reminds us that **joy is found not in taking, but in giving; not in hoarding, but in sharing.** It is in knowing our strength and our responsibility to society that we truly contribute to the global good. Too often, we suggest change to others without realizing that the true change begins with us. The more we are aware of our inner light, the more we illuminate the world around us. When we live with awareness and selflessness, we make a difference—not just in our lives, but in the lives of those we touch.

When you no longer seek the approval of the world, the divine light within you begins to shine for all to see. Let us not merely admire Swamiji's path—let us live it, embody it, and allow it to guide us in every step we take. True greatness is not in recognition, but in the quiet and humble act of living in alignment with higher truth. When we relinquish our desire to be seen, the world sees the best of us—the divine essence that transcends all labels, roles, and expectations. Let us walk the path of selflessness, serving not for applause but for the upliftment of all.

Let us not just admire his path, but walk it. Let us make his teachings a part of our daily lives and, in doing so, transform our surroundings. Swamiji's life reminds us that even the smallest act of kindness, when done with awareness and sincerity, can change the world. When we live simply and selflessly, we not only honor Swamiji's legacy, but we also light the way for others to do the same.

Gurudeva Datta,

We bow to you with open hearts.

You are the light that shows us the way,

Guide us through life, every day.

You didn't run from the world's pain,

But went deeper to heal, again and again.

Help us face our struggles with strength and care,

With love in our hearts, and truth to share.

Teach us to give, not to take,

To live with kindness for all's sake.

Show us the way to serve with grace,

In every moment, in every place.

Gurudeva Datta,

We trust in your wisdom, we follow your light.

Help us live with truth, love, and right.

May your guidance lead us to the highest way,

With every step, come what may.

Gurudeva Datta.

Gurudeva Datta.

Gurudeva Datta.

A MESSAGE FROM HIS HOLINESS SRI VIDYANARAYANA THEERTHA

(For the readers of Waves of Wisdom)

Swamy lovingly shares the following message with all readers of Waves of Wisdom. In his own simple and powerful way, Swamy speaks to the heart of humanity—reminding us of the one truth that unites all beings. May these words inspire reflection, compassion, and a deeper understanding of life.

———•———

"God is One. Truth is God."

In today's modern world, people still fight and hurt each other. There is hate, anger, jealousy, and fear. Science and technology have made great progress, but instead of bringing people together, we are moving further apart. Compassion is disappearing. Kindness is rare. We often forget to love and respect one another.

In every religion, there have been divine souls who came to guide us. Lord Jesus, Prophet Muhammad, Lord Krishna, Lord Rama — each of them was a messenger of love and peace. They lived meaningful lives, showed the path of truth and compassion, and returned to the eternal source after completing their divine work.

Jesus, who suffered deeply, was crucified for his unwavering love and compassion. Despite the betrayal, he forgave those who caused him pain, praying for their ignorance. His life was filled with purity, service, and divine compassion, a message of forgiveness even in the face of unimaginable suffering.

Prophet Muhammad, too, faced persecution, violence, and exile. Yet, he never wavered in his love for humanity. His mission was not just to deliver a message, but to live it, showing forgiveness and compassion, even to those who rejected him.

Lord Krishna, in the Bhagavad Gita, shared the timeless wisdom of surrender, duty, and inner love. His life, too, was one of sacrifice, of guiding others even when the world seemed in chaos. He gave us the gift of love and the strength to endure hardships, teaching us that love and surrender to the Divine are our highest duties.

Great saints like Sri Raghavendra Swamy and Shirdi Sai Baba lived for the well-being of all. They did not see differences between people. They saw the divine in everyone. They didn't just talk about truth — they lived it every day. They were living examples of unconditional love, patience, and forgiveness.

Raghavendra Swamy, once offered objectionable food by a Nawab, responded not with anger, but with divine grace. He transformed the offering into flowers and fruits. It was not about the miracle — it was about the message: Forgiveness is strength. Love is divinity. Peace is power.

We must ask ourselves — what is the use of reading scriptures or praising saints if we do not follow their path? Their lives were their teachings.

Religion is not about names or rituals.

It is the practice of truth, love, and kindness.

Caste is not birth-based.

It is about the purity of thought, word, and action.

One who serves, who uplifts others, who walks in dharma — that is the true noble soul.

Let us stop dividing. Let us start uniting. Let us go beyond language, caste, community, or creed. Let us be good human beings. Let us live with compassion. Let us walk with love. Let us speak with gentleness.

My message is simple —

Love all. Serve all. Be good. Do good.

Forgive and forget. Be kind. Be human.

That is the true wave of wisdom.

– Sri Vidyanarayana Theertha